Worship for All Seasons

Selections from *Gathering* for
- Pentecost
- Summer
- Autumn

Volume
3

edited by
Thomas Harding

THE UNITED CHURCH PUBLISHING HOUSE

Canadian Cataloguing in Publication Data

Main entry under title:

Worship for all seasons

Contents: v. 3. Selections from Gathering for
Pentecost, summer, autumn.
ISBN 1-55134-012-7 (v. 1) ISBN 1-55134-014-3 (v. 3)

1. United Church of Canada — Liturgy — Texts.
2. Worship programs. I. Harding, Thomas Reginald,
1944- .

BX9881.W67 1993   264'.0792   C93-094380-5

The United Church Publishing House
85 St. Clair Avenue East
Toronto, Ontario
M4T 1M8

Publisher: R.L. Naylor
Editor-in-Chief: Peter Gordon White
Project Editor: Elizabeth Phinney
Book Design: Christopher Dumas, Dept. of Graphics and Print
Music Typography: Ann Turner
Printed in Canada by: Best/Gagné Book Manufacturers

5 4 3 2 1 94 95 96 97 98

CONTENTS

INTRODUCTION

A season of celebration! The United Church celebrates the enrichment of its life through the contribution of the worship packet, *Getting It All Together*, edited by George James, and its successor, *Gathering*. We celebrate the artistic contribution of Marilyn James in the cover art. Poetry, hymns, prayers, drama—many reasons for celebration.

Worship for All Seasons is an offering of previously published "home-made" liturgical materials, all of which have been used by children, clergy, musicians, worship committees in the United Church at worship.

The varied themes and observances of the Summer/Autumn period supply many foci for the worship planner. Those who use the Revised Common Lectionary will note that the readings suggested bear slight, if any, relation to one another. The Lectionary planners intentionally permit the Mosaic narrative to unfold sequentially in Year A; the Davidic narrative and the stories of the Prophets do likewise in Years B and C. Old Testament readings are not necessarily aligned with the gospel passages in this period.

The United Church expresses other dimensions of its life and mission during this period through observance of Environment Sunday, First Nations Day of Prayer, Thanksgiving, Peace Sabbath, and oftentimes Anniversary Sunday. This series celebrates the degree of variety and inspiration to be found in the many colours of "Ordinary Time."

As the Spirit has graced those whose gifts appear in this series, may the gift of the Holy Spirit abide in all we are, in all we think and do. A reason for celebration!

Every step has been taken to obtain information about the copyright status of the materials included. All of the material in this book is protected by copyright. It may be used, however, for the purposes of congregational worship without payment of any fee. If an error is detected, the reader is welcome to contact the editor so that corrections can be made. With regard to prayers, the reader is reminded that prayer belongs to the church, and authorship of printed prayers becomes easily blurred.

In this three-volume series, materials are divided according to the seasons of the church year. In each section, information introducing the season, a variety of special services, ideas, and resources, and a selection of hymns may be found. Prayers for special days and festivals are grouped together; prayers of a general nature round out each section.

Emphasis is placed on the fact that the prayer materials in particular are models for adaptation in light of local circumstances, needs, and spirituality. A comment on the prayers: The first is that some are written for more than one voice and are thus delineated: 1. (one voice) and 2. (other voices). Occasionally 1. and 2. indicate two individual voices, with the congregation joining in a refrain. There is no reason, of course, why in some of the prayers, 1. and 2. could not be left side and right side of the congregation, or choir and people.

The reader may find it useful to gain an overview of what pertains to a whole season and note what items, if any, require copyright permission or advance planning. It is usually appropriate to identify the authors of the words used publicly even when copyright notice is not required.

Of further interest will be the first chapter of volume 1 in this series, "Patterns of Worship in The United Church of Canada."

Leitourgia: liturgy: the work of the people. What has been "gathered" has already been the work of some people. May your worship planning and worship life be a blessing as the work of your people unfolds to the glory of God.

Fred Kimball Graham
The Worship Office
Lent, 1994

Chapter
One

Pentecost and the Summer

ABOUT PENTECOST

Pentecost is the festival of the windy, fiery Spirit of God, perhaps the most imagistic of all the Christian festivals. And that is the way it should be celebrated: with images, poetry, dance, and song. Originally a spring harvest festival, Pentecost (also known as the Feast of Weeks) was fifty (Greek *pentakonta*) days after Passover and celebrated the giving of the Law on Mount Sinai.

The colour of Pentecost is red, signifying the "tongues of fire" which rested on each disciple, transforming those who follow (disciples) into those who are sent forth (apostles). Red is also the colour of martyrdom, foreshadowing what was in store for the early Christians ... and for so many who have come after. This Spirit can be a dangerous thing!

L/E/P, 1990

For Christians, Pentecost celebrates the presence of the Holy Spirit in our lives and in the church. We recall the promise made by the risen Christ that he would send a comforter, a source of power, a counsellor (Luke 24:49, Acts 1:1-9, John 15:26, 16:7-15). Pentecost is also celebrated as the birthday of the church (imagine, 1,950-plus birthday candles!).

Always we run into problems when we try to talk about God. The subject is too great for our limited comprehension, not to mention the limits of our language. In Hebrew scripture two of the ways of talking about God's presence were to use images of wind and fire. The disciples at Pentecost used this same imagery to attempt to describe the powerful, moving, invisible yet so real experience of God's Spirit.

Think about your experiences of wind: a cooling breeze on a hot summer day; the force which hoists a kite, drives a sailboat, dries the clothes on a line; the power which sways the trees, hurls the snow, drives the waves onto the beach. We can't see it, but we certainly can experience it.

In Hebrew the word used for "wind" *(ruach)* was also used for "breath" or "spirit." The opening verse of Genesis employs a word-play when it speaks of the spirit (wind) of God moving over the face of the waters. In Genesis 2:7 God breathes into the first person the breath (spirit) of life. In Ezekiel 37:1-14 there is a dramatic tale of a valley of dry bones becoming living beings through the power of God's breath (wind, spirit). In the Gospel of John the gifting of the Spirit occurs when Jesus breathes on his disciples (in Greek, *pneuma* can also mean spirit, wind, or breath).

Think also of your experiences of fire: a single candle in a dark room, a cozy fireplace on a wintry night, burning the leaves in autumn, a campfire for roasting hot dogs and marshmallows or for gathering around for singing. But think also of the terrible destruction of a forest fire, and how we experience just a twinge of worry when a fire truck races by.

In scripture, fire is a particularly potent symbol of God's presence. Moses recognized God's presence in the burning bush and took off his shoes out of reverence (Ex. 3:1-6). Mount Sinai smoked with fire and lightening when the Law was given (Ex. 19:16ff, much to Cecil B. De Mille's delight!) The Elijah stories are full of fire imagery: with the priests of Baal (I Kings 18:30-40), striking the soldiers of Ahaziah (II Kings 1) and, of course, the fiery chariot (II Kings 2:11). Isaiah's call is seared onto his lips with a burning coal (Isa. 6:6-7), and Isaiah himself uses images of fire in warning Israel of coming destruction and their need to be refined in the fire.

The images of wind and fire powerfully describe the windy, fiery Spirit of God.

Susan Lindenberger, 1991

IDEAS AND RESOURCES FOR PENTECOST AND THE SUMMER

The Story of Pentecost in Two Voices

A. This is the day of Pentecost, the day on which we celebrate the birthday of the church, the day on which the disciples received such a startlingly new experience of the presence of God that they were empowered to become the Church of Jesus Christ, a community of new people with a message of good news for a tired and hurting world.

B. The power they received is called the Holy Spirit. In Hebrew scripture it is known as the "wind" or "breath" of God, that presence of God that fills the earth and brings it to birth.

A. Genesis 1: "At the beginning of creation, when God made the heavens and the earth, the earth was without form and void, with darkness over the face of the deep. But a mighty wind, a God-wind, swept over the surface of the waters...."

B. The wind of God, that presence which inflates the world and people full to overflowing with life.

A. Genesis 2: "Then God formed a person from the dust of the ground, and breathed into the person's nostrils the breath of life. And the person became a living being."

B. A God-wind blew...

A. ... and the world had life!

B. God breathed the breath of God's Spirit...

A. ... and the first person came alive!

B. Listen while the choir sings a song about the Spirit that is loose in the world.... ("Spirit of God in the clear-running water," by the Medical Mission Sisters).

***

A. A story from the gospel according to St. John: One night a learned Pharisee came to Jesus asking, "Teacher, how can a person enter God's new community?"

B. "In truth, in very truth I tell you, unless you are born again you cannot be part of God's new community. Flesh gives birth to flesh, but it is Spirit that gives birth to spirit. That is what it means to be born again.
"You are puzzled, but I tell you, the wind blows where it wills; you hear the sound of it but you do not know where it comes from or where it is going. That is the way it is when you are born of the wind of the Spirit!"

A. To be born of the wind of the Spirit. That is what it means to be the Pentecost people of God.

B. "Spirit, Spirit of gentleness": Let us sing it together.... (*Songs for a Gospel People,* no. 108).

***

3

A.   After the resurrection, the disciples waited in Jerusalem for the promised gift of the Spirit. Hear how the church was born:

B.   "While the day of Pentecost was running its course, they were all together in one place. Suddenly there came from the sky a noise like that of a strong, rushing wind, a wind which filled the whole house. They were set on fire with what appeared to be tongues of flame, resting on each one of them. And they were filled with the Holy Spirit."

A.   Jesus had told them to wait for the Spirit, and they had waited. Now, gathered together in a house, suddenly they knew what it meant to be the church. Filled with the presence of God they were born again, born of the wind of the Spirit, ready and willing to be blown out into a world that so desperately needed new people for a new age.

B.   We have gathered this morning, as the disciples were gathered nineteen hundred and fifty years ago, waiting for the Spirit. Can we be filled with the winds of God?

A.   We can if we will but let ourselves go, if we will but let our church go, and be swept along by the winds of God.

B.   We can if we will but let ourselves go, if we will but let our church go, and be swept along by the winds of God.

A.   "I feel the winds of God today, today my sail I lift": Let's sing it together.... (*The Hymn Book,* no. 282).

***

B.   What does it mean to be filled with God's Holy Spirit? We close with the words of St. Paul:

A.   "For the harvest of the Spirit is love, joy, peace, patience, kindness, goodness, faithfulness, gentleness, and self-control. There is no law dealing with such things as these; they are the fruit of the Spirit. If, then, the Spirit is the source of our life, let the Spirit also direct our course."

B.   "If, then, the Spirit is the source of our life, let the Spirit also direct our course." May God give us grace to be the Pentecost people of God.

A.   Let us pray silently for a moment, and then quietly sing, remaining seated, "Breathe on me, Breath of God" (*The Hymn Book,* no. 240).

Beaverlodge United, Beaverlodge, Alta., 1978

Pentecost in Many Voices

We used scripture reading and a litany-sermon at Summerland United during an intergenerational service. The scripture reading and the litany portions of the sermon were designed to spread the reading and preaching throughout the entire worshipping community.

The congregation was invited to read together the scripture reading from Acts 2. This was printed on two coloured inserts (we used red and gold to match the colours of Pentecost). The two inserts had similar versions of the reading so that, as we began to read of "speaking in different tongues," we began to say different words, although with the same meaning. Then, as the reading spoke of the "crowds marvelling," and "each sharing and understanding," the reading became unison once again. As the reading then focuses on Peter as spokesperson for the disciples, we continued with a single reader. In this way, something of the drama of the event was re-created.

The sermon was in three parts, with a portion of the congregation reading a litany of the Spirit's presence in wind, fire, and the gift of tongues. The preacher then followed each litany with a brief reflection on the biblical images of wind, fire, and the giving of gifts for the unity and building up of the body. Each meditation took two to three minutes.

Throughout, there was a feeling of lightness and movement. The banners were free-hanging crêpe paper streamers in red, orange, and gold, which caught every movement of air. The flow between preacher and congregation, and from one part of the congregation to another, gave the entire service a feeling of the Spirit's presence, "distributed and resting on each one." The litanies were as follows:

We are people of the Spirit;
we are formed by the wind.
The breath of God gave life to the first human being;
the winds of the Spirit blew over the valley of the dry
    bones and brought life.
"The wind blows where it wills, and you hear the
    sound of it,
but you do not know whence it comes or whither it
    goes;
so it is with everyone who is born of the Spirit."
Without the wind of the Spirit we are like a sail
on a dead quiet day:
    stale, empty, useless.
A mighty rushing wind came from heaven
    to fill the disciples with the Spirit.
Send your breath, your wind, O God of Pentecost,
    to fill us and stir us to be people of the Spirit.

We are people of the Spirit;
we are found by fire.
The flames of God flickering in the burning bush
    found and called Moses.
The pillar of flame and smoke
    guided Israel through the wilderness.
Jesus came to baptize us with the Holy Spirit and
    with fire.
Without the flames of the Spirit we are like unlit
    candles:
    cold, dark, useless.
"There appeared to them tongues as of fire,
    distributed and resting on each one of them."
Send your flames, your fire, O God of Pentecost,
    to light us and stir us to be people of the Spirit.

We are people of the Spirit;
we have been gifted by the Spirit's touch.
The Spirit gives to us the words we preach,
    the music we sing, the prayers we offer.
The Spirit gives to us the love we show,
    the faith we teach, the hope we share.
The Spirit is here in every breath, in every spark,
    in our words and our silences, our speaking and
        our hearing.
Send your gifts, your grace, O God of Pentecost,
    to give us power to be people of the Spirit.

Summerland United, Summerland, B.C., 1988

Peter, the Pentecost Balloon

Once upon a time, long, long ago, there was a balloon. His name was Peter. He lived in a house made of plastic along with many other balloons. His house actually had a special name. It was called an "Assorted Pack," which meant that there were balloons of every colour and size in the neighbourhood.

Some, like Peter, had letters painted on them. And that's how they got their names: There was Heidi, the Happy Birthday Balloon; Mary, the Merry Christmas Balloon; Harold, the Happy New Year Balloon; Annie, the Anniversary Balloon; and Peter, well, he had the strangest writing of them all! On his body there was not happy something or merry something; it simply said, "Pentecost." Nobody really knew what it meant. Big Sidney the Sigma Beta Phi Balloon thought that the word meant "fiftieth" in Greek. But no one could really tell poor Peter what the fiftieth stood for. So Peter the Pentecost Balloon just continued living in his house of plastic called "Assorted."

Life was pretty boring there, you know. It's not much fun living with a bunch of balloons. They all looked so dull, flat as a prairie field. Nothing exciting ever happened. Sure, they got to watch television once in a while through those sheer plastic windows, but what's so exciting about watching grown men chasing a funny little piece of black rubber all over a slippery white surface? Peter the Pentecost Balloon went on hoping that something exciting would happen to him. Oh how he longed to discover what his name meant! Oh how he yearned to discover the world outside his assorted house of plastic!

Well, the days went by as slowly as Canada Post's delivery; until one day, finally, Peter the Pentecost Balloon's wish came true. First of all, somebody grabbed him by the neck and held him tightly between two pink mounds of flesh. His heart began beating fast; he could feel his body stretch all over. "Oh my gosh," he thought, "what's happening to me? Whoever's gotta hold on me is really causing a tremendous transformation in me. I've never felt this way before. What's happening?"

Suddenly he felt the grip on his neck slacken. And before you knew it, he was flying all over the room. He had never been so high in all his life (if you know what I mean). He was filled with ecstasy. But then, after a while, he came down. He didn't feel high any more. It seemed like he'd hit the ground. But no sooner had he landed than a hand picked him up and made him swell again. This time, whoever held him suddenly opened his mouth a little bit, still holding him by the neck. And Peter the Pentecost balloon began to speak and shout and sing, although he had no idea whatsoever what he was saying and why. It must have something to do with whatever they do to me when they blow into me, he thought.

But soon the talking and singing came to an end as well. Once again, somebody began blowing more air into him. This time, though, after causing him to expand, they tied a string around his neck. Peter thought he would fly. But no, he didn't fly. Peter thought he might sing in a strange language. But no, he didn't sing.

Instead Peter found himself in the hands of a little child. She touched him, threw him up in the air, caught him when he came down, rolled him across the carpet, chased him all over the room. Peter wasn't sure about all this bouncing about. But then he heard someone say, "Look how much Tracy is enjoying the balloon! That Pentecost balloon has been the best thing to comfort Tracy ever since she lost her mother." Peter the Pentecost Balloon was very happy. So what if he couldn't fly or speak in strange tongues! He was more useful here comforting this little child.

Peter stayed with Tracy for several days, until one day, he went along with Tracy to a strange place. There were lots of people and children there. And whaddyaknow! There were also lots of other balloons. And, a funny thing, they all had the word Pentecost written on them. "What could this place be?" he thought. "What would you call a place that is filled with Pentecost balloons?" And then he heard Tracy whisper to him, "This is the church, Peter. These Pentecost balloons are filled with the Holy Spirit."

And the minister said, "Let us join in singing 'I am the church, you are the church, we are the church together.'" And Peter the Pentecost Balloon began to dance with all the kids and all the other folks, and all the other balloons in the church.

Jeeva Sam, 1988

A Dramatized Reading of John 3:1-16

This reading requires three sets of characters: 1. Jesus and Nicodemus, in period costume, *mime* the story from the chancel steps, freezing as the readers read; 2. NICODEMUS and JESUS *read* the story from the pulpit; 3. A, B, and C *comment* on the story from the lectern (perhaps in black gowns).

(Jesus enters, sniffs the night air, stretches, then seats himself.)

NIC: John writes in the third chapter of his gospel: Now there was a Pharisee named Nicodemus, a leader of the Jews. He came to Jesus by night....

(Nicodemus enters cautiously and makes his way toward Jesus. He hesitates....)

A: An important man. An educated man. A man of authority.

B: If he's so important, why all the caution?

A: Well, someone in *his* position can't be seen chatting with a travelling evangelist.

C: Look for the truth beneath that truth. Do you remember how often John uses the images of darkness and light? It is not simply from the darkness of a spring evening that Nicodemus moves.

(Nicodemus moves toward Jesus and makes a slight gesture of greeting, such as waving his right hand to and away from his forehead.)

NIC: Rabbi, we know that you are a teacher who has come from God; for no one can do these signs that you do apart from the presence of God.

A: Like others, Nicodemus is impressed by the mighty deeds done by this Galilean rabbi.

B: Unlike the sight-seers, Nicodemus knows that the source is more important than the signs.

A: Many flocked to Jesus because of the miracles.

B: Many fled when the miracles failed to bring in the new order they sought.

C: The visitor's overture is polite—but Jesus ignores it.

(Jesus half rises with a similar gesture of greeting.)

JES: Very truly, I tell you, no one can see the kingdom of God without being born anew.

(Jesus gestures for Nicodemus to sit. He does.)

A: "See" the kingdom of God? Encounter, experience, participate in the kingdom of God? The word means all these things.

B: But *what* does it mean?

C: No wonder Nicodemus stalls for time.

NIC: How can anyone be born after having grown old? Can a person enter a second time into his or her mother's womb and be born anew?

B: Don't believe for a minute that this Nicodemus is making an obstetrical inquiry.

C: Maybe he knows he's getting answers to questions he isn't ready to ask.

A: *Maybe* he's wishing he'd stayed in that cool Jerusalem dusk, hearing the swish of olive branches without seeking the source of the sound.

JES: Very truly, I tell you, no one can enter the kingdom of God without being born of water and Spirit.

A: The kingdom of God, again.

B: This kingdom cannot be admired just for its signs, marvellous though they be.

C: The kingdom must be entered, even as this world of sunsets and olive trees is entered—by birth. The dark, wet womb must be left behind.

A: The breaking waters of the womb become the water of our baptism.

B: The Holy Spirit is our midwife.

C: And we are born into God's new order. We join God's shalom community.

(Jesus stands.)

JES: What is born of the flesh is flesh, and what is born of the Spirit is spirit. Do not be astonished that I said to you: You must be born anew.

A: But we *are* astonished.

B: We thought we were doing just fine.

C: We keep the law, go to church on Sunday, bring non-perishable items for the food bank.

A: We spend a lot of time and money on spirituality: books, workshops, spiritual advisors. We truly want to add the Spirit to our crowded, empty lives.

B: Some of us are already born-again Christians. We have claimed Jesus as our own. Surely *we* have the Spirit.

JES: The wind blows where it wills, and you hear the sound of it; but you do not know where it comes from or where it goes. *(Jesus sits.)* So it is with all who are born of the Spirit.

NIC: How can these things be?

A: Still bewildered, Nicodemus?

B: Still in the dark?

C: Or are you wishing you could *return* to the dark—the warm, comfortable womb?

A: For, having seen this much of the light, you cannot return to total darkness again.

B: Always the light will invade your night.

C: Always you will hear the wind, sometimes whispering...

A: ... sometimes howling, shaking at your windows.

B: Will you simply *hear* the wind, wondering where it comes from, where it goes?

C: Or will you listen with held breath, and *enter* the wind, and let it surround you, breathe into you, breathe through you?

A: Still in the dark, Nicodemus?

JES: Are you a teacher of Israel and yet you do not understand these things? Very truly, I tell you, we speak of what we know and testify to what we have seen; yet you do not receive our testimony. If I have told you about earthly things and you do not believe, how can you believe if I tell you about heavenly things?

A: And Nicodemus makes no answer....

(All characters freeze ... and then quietly retire.)

Susan Lindenberger, 1987

"Who Is This God Guy Anyway?": A Dialogue for Trinity Sunday

1. Why in heaven's name is this first Sunday after Pentecost called Trinity Sunday?

2. Because we believe in a "triune" God, one God in three "persons"—because, historically, Christians have experienced God as "Father," "Son," and "Holy Spirit."

1. I see, the One *beyond* us, the One *with* us, and the One *within* us.

2. Hey, that's pretty good! The word "trinity" also tells us that our God, the Maker of heaven and earth,

1. the Source, Sustainer, and Renewer of all creation, the Judge and Redeemer of us all—this God has many sides, many faces, many names.

2. We see God especially in the person of Jesus of Nazareth, the one we confess as God's Anointed One, in Hebrew "Messiah" or in Greek "Christ."

1. The first Christians saw Jesus as the "Son" of God, the "Word" of God,

2. and the "Lamb" of God.

1. In the Bible, Jesus is also called the Way, the Truth and the Life,

2. the Prince of Peace, the Holy One, Saviour, Anchor,

1. Shepherd and Bishop of Souls, Lion of the tribe of Judah.

2. The Author and Finisher of our faith, the Bread of Life, the True Vine, the Chief Cornerstone, Rabbi.

1. The Sun of Righteousness, the Bright and Morning Star.

2. The Son of Man, the King of Kings,

1. Living Water, Righteous Judge,

2. Head of the Church, Light of the World, Horn of Salvation,

1. Alpha and Omega, Redeemer, Lord of All.

2. Down through the centuries, Christians have continued to call Jesus by many names, by *new* names.

1. For instance, the German pastor-theologian, Dietrich Bonhoeffer (who was executed by the Nazis), called Jesus "the man for others."

2. From Babe of Bethlehem, to Suffering-Servant, to Risen Lord, Jesus has meant many things to many people.

1. Because in him we see the human face of God.

2. In him we see the God of utter faithfulness, of radical justice, the God of infinite mercy, compassionate power, and unconditional love.

1. So how can one name alone describe this God?

2. Exactly! One name is not enough.

***

1. Now, even though it's Trinity Sunday, it is also the Season of Pentecost.

2. And so we also proclaim the power and presence of the Spirit who moves within us and among us.

1. To try and express the many-sided concern of God *for* us, the biblical writers resorted to a number of ideas and images for the Spirit.

2. All of these were attempts to describe the ways in which people have experienced God as *Spirit*—felt God as a disturbing power or driving force in their lives.

1. As Jesus told Nicodemus, God's Spirit breathes, as the wind blows, freely—where it wills.

2. It was God's Spirit, breathed into us (as we know from Genesis) that first gave us life.

1. In the book of Ezekiel it says that the Spirit of the Lord falls upon certain people and makes them prophets and witnesses to God's word.

2. It also says that the Spirit can turn hearts of stone into hearts of flesh.

1. In the Gospels, God's Spirit descends on Jesus like a dove at the beginning of his public ministry.

2. The Spirit is also given to the disciples, and at Pentecost, it comes to the gathered people of God like a wind-storm and like fire.

1. In various places in the New Testament the Spirit is sent by God (as Jesus promised) to be "Advocate," "Guide," or "Governor."

2. The One who counsels and comforts us.

1. So the Spirit of God is compared to natural forces and human functions that are familiar to us.

2. Even though people in the early church knew that the power of the Spirit could never be fully captured in the words or pictures used to describe it.

***

1. So, in the Bible God has many names.

2. God is likened to a warrior, a lord, a king, a master, a judge, a shield, a fortress, a strong man excited by wine, and a sword-wielder....

1. Ah, excuse me. But isn't that all a bit, well, *war-like*?

2. Sure. But then again, God is also portrayed as a bridegroom, a husband, a father....

1. Sorry to interrupt again, but aren't those images all, well, terribly *masculine*?

2. So?

1. Well, aren't you forgetting something?

2. I don't think so ... no, wait. God is not only given male names in the Bible. God is also compared to natural objects and events, like a never-failing stream, a thundering voice, a consuming and purifying fire. He's also called "the Rock of our salvation," and a Lion.

1. Yes, but that's not quite what I was getting at.

2. Well?

1. The Bible says that God has another side—a *feminine* side!

2. What?

1. Yes, God is only *sometimes* like a male warrior. Other times, God is like a lover, a shepherd, a potter, a baker-woman, a hen, a mother eagle, a womb, a she-bear robbed of her cubs.

2. Those are in the Bible?

1. Sure are. And there are other examples. God's wisdom, for instance, is personified in many places as a *woman*. The Hebrew word for "spirit" is *feminine* in gender. Remember the first verse of Genesis? In the beginning, the wind or spirit of God *broods* over the face of the waters.

2. Say, that's interesting. The first image for God in the Bible is of a mother bird stirring up and sheltering the stuff of creation.

1. "As an eagle stirs up her nest, flutters over her young, spreads her wings, takes them up, bears them aloft on her pinions: So the Lord alone guided them." That's from Deuteronomy, chapter 32.

2. Well, that's one more example.

1. It's also found in Exodus, chapter 19; Ruth, chapter 2; Psalms 17, 57, 61, 91....

2. Okay, okay!

1. There's more, you know. In Psalm 22:9-10, God is a midwife.

2. Maybe so. But I still say the best images for God are strong ones. God *is* called "Rock" you know, and that's a pretty masculine-sounding description.

1. "You were unmindful of the Rock that bore you, you forgot the God who gave you birth...." That's Deuteronomy 32:18. I don't know many *men* who have given birth—do you?

2. Not lately, anyway. But look, we're not supposed to take the idea of God giving birth *literally*, are we?

1. Of course not. But we should take the idea *seriously*, because it reveals something true about the nature of God.

2. You mean it tells us that God is not male.

1. More than that—it tells us that in many ways God is like a *woman.*

2. Now that you mention it, I remember places in the New Testament where the activity of God is compared to that of a baker-woman (Matt. 13:33; Luke 13:20-21) and a homemaker who seeks out what is lost (Luke 15:8-10). And I guess that when Jesus says that we must be born again, he doesn't mean birth from our mother's womb, but from the womb of God's Spirit!

1. I think that's right.

2. But I'm not used to thinking about God as having a womb.

1. Not many people are. But it's a biblical image.

2. You have some more examples, I suppose?

1. Need you ask? How's this? God says: "From the beginning I have been silent, I have kept quiet, held myself in check. But now I will groan like a woman in labour, I will gasp and pant."

2. *God* said that?

1. In Isaiah 42:14. Look it up.

2. I believe you. God can be like a woman giving birth. I guess that's a good way of describing God as the Creator of nature. Creation comes forth out of God's womb. Job 38, verses 28-29, would be an example.

1. Right. But, you know, the Bible talks of God as the Lord of history as well as of nature; and here too it refers to God's womb. You see, the Hebrew word for "womb" is the same as the word for "compassion." So all the references

to God's mercy or compassion for us could also be translated as the protective, nourishing "womb-love" of God, our Divine Mother. In Jeremiah 31:15-22, God speaks like a merciful mother to her child, Israel.

2. I see what you mean. I remember a passage in Isaiah where God reassures Israel that he will not forsake his children.

1. Right, it's in Isaiah 49, verse 15; and given the imagery, maybe you should say that God will not forsake *her* children.

2. Touché! God says, "Can a woman forget the baby sucking at her breast, that she should have no compassion on the son of her womb? I will not forget you." But you know, somehow I don't remember the Bible being so *sexually explicit* when talking about God.

1. I hope you don't find it too embarrassing, because it gets worse.

2. No!

1. Yes—the Bible doesn't pussyfoot around. In Genesis 49:25 the name given to the Lord in Hebrew is "Shaddai."

2. So?

1. It comes from a root word originally meaning "breast."

2. Go on!

1. I mean it. Read Isaiah 66, verses 9, 12, 13, 14. God is described as a *nursing mother* who comforts her baby.

2. I suppose that's just one isolated passage?

1. No, look up Hosea 11:4. God's a nursing mother there too. Later on, in Hosea 13, God says she will react to the infidelity of the people she saved like a mother bear who loses her cubs.

2. All right. I surrender. God is a lot bigger than any box we try to shut him or her up in.

1. That's why the Bible uses different kinds of images for God. Even in the apocryphal book of Second Esdras (which dates from New Testament times) God is portrayed in the *same* passage as a father, a mother, and a wet-nurse.

2. Let me read it: "Thus says the Almighty God, have I not prayed for you as a *father* his sons, as a *mother* her daughters, and a *nurse* her young babes, that you would be my people, and I should be your God...? (2 Esdras 1:28-9).

1. The point is that our Lord and Maker is neither a male God nor a female Goddess, but *Yahweh,* the One who is, who was, and who ever shall be—the One who calls everything into being.

2. So God has no gender. In Exodus 3:14, in the story of the burning bush, Moses is told God's true name: "Yahweh," which means simply "I Am." So God says *I am who I am; I cause everything to be; I will be who I will be.*

1. This is a God beyond our understanding, but whose nature is love.

2. To this God be the glory! Amen.

Paul Fayter, 1986

A Litany of Thanksgiving at the Close of Church School

MINISTER: From the expectations of last fall, through the joy of Thanksgiving, the expectation of Advent, the wonder of Christmas, the reflective time of Lent, the celebration of Easter, our Sunday school has come.

STUDENTS AND TEACHERS: We give thanks to God for opportunities for learning, for experiencing friendship, for growing in faith and love.

CONGREGATION: And we give thanks to God for all your hard work and for the joy you have found in each other and the joy you have brought to us.

STUDENTS: We thank God for our teachers and for the fun, crafts, and special days in church, and for the friends we have made.

TEACHERS: We thank God for good resources and for helpful youngsters, for time to prepare, and for the rewards that come from teaching.

MINISTER: We thank God for a wise and caring superintendent, and for all those whose gifts have been shared in our church school this year.

CONGREGATION: We thank God for a time of rest and relaxation now that summer is here and we pray for those who will lead our summer church school.

ALL: God, whose Word is truth, whose presence is joy, and whose promises are for all people of all ages: We ask your blessing on our whole church as together we strive to be your people in this place.

David Sparks, 1990

The Story of Moses with Children

In Year A of the *Common Lectionary,* a major series of Hebrew scripture readings throughout the summer and fall focuses on the story of Moses. Construct a large map. Trace the story each week on the map and tape an appropriate symbol (e.g., bulrush, burning bush, stone tablets) to mark the spot on which the story took place. Each week have a different person or family from the congregation tell the story as if they had been there:

Exodus 1:6-14, 22-2:10: Miriam tells how she and her mother hid her baby brother Moses and fooled the Egyptians.

Exodus 2:11-22: Zipporah tells of why Moses had to flee Egypt, how he met her in Midian, and how they got married.

Exodus 3:1-12: Moses recounts the experience of the burning bush (note especially his feelings of fear and awe).

Exodus 3:13-20: Moses gets further instructions from God, but protests that he is inadequate to the task.

Exodus 12:1-14: Aaron tells the story of the Passover.

Exodus 14:19-31: Miriam tells of the crossing of the Sea of Reeds (note Miriam's Song in Exodus 15:20-21).

Exodus 16:2-15: An Israelite family (Levi, Ruth, Jacob, and Leah) tell about God's gift of manna in the wilderness.

Exodus 17:1-7: An older person or couple remembers the gift of water from the rock.

Exodus 19:1-9: Moses speaks to God, who tells him what to say to the Israelites.

Exodus 19:16-24: An Israelite family tells of the storm and the huge mountain, and how only Moses was allowed to go up the mountain.

Exodus 20:1-20: Moses recites the Ten Commandments.

Exodus 32:1-14: Aaron tells of creating the golden calf, having given in to the pressure of the people.

Exodus 33:12-23: Moses tells of seeing the "backside" of God. Or juggle the readings so that Deuteronomy 8:7-18 is read (instead of Exodus 33) on Thanksgiving Sunday. Miriam tells of the long period of the wilderness wanderings and talks about thanksgiving (note especially Deuteronomy 8:17-18).

Numbers 27:12-23: Joshua tells of his commissioning by Moses.

Deuteronomy 34:1-12: Joshua tells of the death of Moses and reflects on Moses' life (note particularly verses 10-12).

Each Sunday, use the psalm (printed and read responsively) as a response to the story. Chose one line that sums up the psalm, have someone set it to a simple tune, teach it to the congregation, and sing it as an antiphon every few verses throughout the reading of the psalm.

Rose Ferries, 1984

"The Friend with a Hearing Problem": A Story

Once there was a hospital patient who refused to allow people to visit him. That had not always been so; in fact, there had been times when he had greatly appreciated the care and empathy shown by his friends. But his attitude changed one day when he was feeling low and a friend dropped in to visit.

When the patient said that he was feeling discouraged, the friend suggested that things would get better. When he said that he was afraid, the friend assured him that there was no reason in the world to be frightened. When he said he was lonely at times, his friend pointed out that there were other patients in the room and that he could talk to them.

When the patient worried that his sickness might be quite serious, the friend reminded him that there were always others worse off than he was. When he said that he was quite worried about a scheduled operation, he received the advice: "Don't worry! You're in good hands."

Finally the patient told his friend that he needed to be alone. When the nurse came in later, he told her that he did not want to have any more visitors.

G. Harvie Barker, 1990

HYMNS FOR PENTECOST AND THE SUMMER

Psalm 104, Pentecost

(Arnsberg, 6 6 8 D 3 3 6 6)

Majesty and splendour,
our Light and Defender,
is the God whose praise we render.
Holy Light abiding,
fire and flame not hiding,
on the wings of wind is riding.
Praise the Lord
with the word of our great rejoicing;
all creation voicing.

How great is your wisdom!
Earth and sky and sea come
hoping,
yearning for your kingdom.
When you send your Spirit
all life is created.
You renew
what once was hated.
Earth shall quake,
mountains shake at the holy glory.
We shall sing the story.

Sylvia Dunstan, 1988

Go to the world!

(*Sine Nomine*, 10 10 10 4)

Go to the world!
Go into all the earth.
Go preach the cross
where Christ renews life's worth,
baptizing as the sign of our rebirth.
Alleluia! Alleluia!

Go to the world!
Go into every place.
Go live the Word
of God's redeeming grace.
Go seek God's presence
in each time and space.
Alleluia!

Go to the world!
Go struggle, bless and pray;
the nights of tears
give way to joyous day.
As servant church,
we follow Christ's own way.
Alleluia!

Go to the world!
Go as the ones I send,
for I am with you
'til the age shall end,
when all the hosts of glory
cry "Amen!"
Alleluia!

Sylvia Dunstan, 1986

Spirit of healing

(Morning is Broken, 10 9 10 9)

Spirit of healing, Spirit of wholeness,
gather your people under your wing.
We who are broken, we the downtrodden,
we seek the comfort only you bring.

Spirit of healing, Spirit of wholeness,
Spirit, you find faith in every soul.
Ten lepers cried out, "Rabbi, please heal us!"
One returned thanks, his faith made him whole.

Spirit of healing, Spirit of wholeness,
like Jairus' daughter you tell us to rise.
Rise from our pallets, rise from our failings,
rise to forgiveness warm in your eyes.

Spirit of healing, Spirit of wholeness,
Christ revealed to us wounds have a worth.
Dying he showed us strength comes from weakness,
his brokenness brings life to all the earth.

Kate Galea, 1990

Holy Spirit, wind and fire

(Stuttgart, Sharon 8 7 8 7)

Holy Spirit, wind and fire,
bringing order to the earth:
move upon chaotic waters,
giving love and life and birth.

Holy Spirit, dove descending,
herald Noah's ebbing flood.
Come to Christ in Jordan's waters—
sin now washed away in blood.

Holy Spirit, peace and passion,
give us tongues to praise the name—
Christ the one above all others,
through the ages still the same.

Holy Spirit, calm our chaos,
give us order in these days.
In the flood and fire and fury,
fill our hearts with endless praise.

Colin Peterson, 1992

Arise, arise, O God of gracious song

(*Sursum Corda*, Ellers, 10 10 10 10)

Arise, arise, O God of gracious song.
Arise in us that we may sing along.
Arise in life that all of life may praise.
Arise in hope, O Maker of our days.

Take flight, take wings, O Spirit of the years.
Take flight in strength and banish all our fears.
Take wings and soar as gentle as a dove.
Take flight in hearts alive to holy love.

Break out, break forth, O Sun of Righteousness.
Break out, break forth and all your people bless.
Break forth, break out in heaven and on earth.
Break free, break free to mark the things of worth.

Shine on, shine on, O holy ones of God.
Shine on, shine on where all the saints have trod.
Shine on, shine on for all the world to see.
Sine on, shine on, and gain your victory.

Malcolm Sinclair, 1987

An Offertory Hymn for Summer

(Forest Green, Kingsfold 8 6 8 6 D)

We praise your name, O Risen Christ,
for life in all its grace:
the fertile land, the summer sun,
your love within this place.
Receive these gifts, our work and bread,
made holy by your hand,
and consecrate us in your way
of peace in all the land.

Rob Johns, 1987

God lives among us

(Maccabaeus, 5 5 6 5 6 5 6 5 and refrain)

God lives among us,
source of life and light,
fountain of our loving,
river of delight.
God's let loose among us:
so our God transcends,
moving us to touch God
as we touch our friends.

Refrain: God lives among us,
source of life and light,
fountain of our living,
river of delight.

Christ comes with justice,
everlasting stream;
calls us as God's partners,
we must heal, redeem;
like a mighty river
rolling to the sea,
generates our power,
frees us to set free.

Refrain....

Wisdom the Spirit,
living water, grace,
welcomes all the thirsty
to her dwelling-place.
Fountain, stream and river
flow throughout the earth,
water where we're desert,
bring new life to birth.

Refrain....

Ruth Evans, 1991

We Are One

It is preferred that this verse be used for communion occasions only.

© 1987 Words by Doreen Lankshear-Smith
P.O. Box 3791, Thunder Bay, ON P7A 6E3
© 1987 Music by Jeeva Sam

A Benediction with Amens

May the grace of Christ at-tend us, and the love of God sur-round us, and the Ho-ly Spi-rit keep us, now and ev-er al-ways, A-men. A-men, for-ev-er and ev-er. A-men.

© 1987, Words & music by Jeeva Sam
154 Sangster Blvd., Regina, SK S4R 6L5
Harmonization: Fred Graham

The Hymn Book as Creative Resource

Pentecost

245 **"Come, Holy Ghost"**
Makes a dramatic choir processional, best when unaccompanied.

247 **"Fire of God"**
A very attractive Pentecost introit.

258 **"Come, my Way"**
Originally written as a solo. I have tried this with the entire choir during communion, in unison and very softly, with suitable interludes between verses.

Summer

2 **"Let all the world"**
A lovely introit! See list of other introits in index at back of the book.

3 **"From all that dwell"**
Also a good introit. Try to the tune of no. 1 (*"Lasst Uns Erfreuen"*).

11 **"Praise the Lord! His glories show"**
Any kind of antiphony is always effective. This has obvious possibilities.

12 **"All people that on earth do dwell"**
Pull out, borrow, or buy the Vaughan Williams version. Use the various harmonizations for variety, or the thrilling, brassy introduction before the doxology on special occasions.

30 **"Praise my soul"**
A ready-made anthem, each verse different in texture, harmony and style.

38 **"Sing ye praises"**
Do learn this as an anthem, then teach it to the congregation. Only two phrases to learn, and such super words and sprightly music.

43 **"Bright the vision"**
Thrilling, with the descant provided!

100 **"O love, how deep"**
This is one of those hymns that can be sung in canon, i.e., as a round, since it keeps the same harmonic rhythm throughout. Try choir alone, in canon, on one verse, and not too slowly—the original was a lively dance.

143 **"When Israel was in Egypt's land"**
The children in the church school would love this one, in conjunction with the Moses story.

146 **"The Church's one foundation"**
Even an oldie like this comes to life with a new tune. Try to no. 447, St. Theodulf.

160 **"O Holy City"**
A powerful anthem, complete with descant.

179 **(St. Albinus) "Jesus lives!"**
A terrific Easter introit, sure to wake 'em up!

186 **"O what their joy"**
Makes a wonderful anthem. If you get hold of Willan's anthem version and tell the choir to watch for their entries but sing from the hymn book, for the price of one anthem you have a magnificent piece for All Saints' or Remembrance Day.

192 **"O Love that wilt not let me go"**
Like anything harmonized by Bach, this becomes a splendid anthem.

249 **"Dear Lord and Father"**
The first tune, "Repton," is so lovely that you really should give "Rest" a rest and introduce this one to all your die-hards. Beautiful as a solo, also.

Lydia Pedersen, 1990

PRAYERS FOR PENTECOST AND THE SUMMER

Greeting and Versicle

The ancient Apostolic greeting, "The grace of our Saviour Christ...," is always appropriate as the initial act of worship. It establishes at the outset in whose name we have gathered, links us to the ancient and ecumenical church (the Greeting has been in use for almost two thousand years), and has the added benefit, when used Sunday by Sunday, of being easily memorized.

On festival days or in special seasons, a scripture versicle may be added after the Greeting. Normally the versicle underscores the theme of the day or season.

1. The grace of our Saviour Christ, the love of God, and the communion of the Holy Spirit be with you all.
2. And also with you.
1. Come, Holy Spirit, and fill the hearts of your faithful.
2. Kindle us with the fire of your love.

Prayers of the Day (Collects)

The Prayer of the Day also underscores the theme of the day or season, perhaps picking up a particular phrase or emphasis from the scripture passages to be read later in the service. (A useful device in providing unity in a service is this technique of foreshadowing or, later in the service, echoing the scripture readings.)

The ancient prayer form of the collect is often used in the Prayer of the Day. The prayer is addressed to God and focuses on God's action and God's praise.

Your Spirit, God, works in our weakness until we are aflame with your love and power. Fill the hearts of your faithful with living fire, that we may set the world ablaze; through Jesus Christ, to whom with you and the Spirit, one holy God, be honour and praise, now and forever.

Sylvia Dunstan, 1988

Pentecostal God: You fulfilled the promise of Easter by gifting your church with the power of your Spirit; you have called us into the church through water and the Spirit, baptizing us into newness of life. Gift us again: Kindle us with love, fulfil your church with power, blow us into the world in the name of your Risen One; to whom with you and the Spirit, one holy God, be honour and praise, now and forever.

Thomas Harding, 1990

O God, whose glory is our hope, whose love is our deepest joy: Open us this morning to the presence of your Spirit and the truth of your gospel, that our lives may be challenged and our faith strengthened; through Jesus the Christ, to whom with you and the Spirit, one holy God, be honour and praise, now and forever.

John McTavish, 1977

By your Spirit, God, you bind all people in human community. Direct us, in our worship, to lose ourselves in thanksgiving and praise, that we might find ourselves in the unity of love which comes through your Beloved Child, Jesus the Christ; to whom, with you and the Spirit, one holy God, be honour and praise, now and forever.

Roland Hutchinson, 1988

O God, in whose mercy we find our peace, in whose presence we find our place, in whose world we find our calling: Grant us grace so to hear and accept your Word that we may be faithful, followers of your will and your way all our days. In Jesus name we pray.

Lynette Miller, 1986

O God, revealed, incarnate and at work among us: Grant to all who gather here minds that are open to perceive you, hearts that are open to receive you, lives that are open to live for you; that we may be the people who both know and live what we believe; through Jesus Christ our Saviour.

S/A, 1987

O God of leafy bough and climbing rose, of azure sky and summer light: Let life abound in our hearts, and let it speak to us of the goodness of creation and the pulsing energy of your great love; through Christ our Saviour.

Peter Wyatt, 1989

God of beauty wounded, whom wind and wave obey: Teach us the way of spendthrift love and extravagant, wild mercy. Pour out your Spirit now on us, that we may serve the world you love with hearts set free. For you alone are God, and blessed is your name.

Paul Fayter, 1991

God of yesterday and of tomorrow: Always you startle us into new understandings just when we think we have it all sorted out. Startle us again. Break open our preconceptions and confound our pat answers, that we might be gifted with new vision. Praise be to you, Surprising One.

Thomas Harding, 1991

God of compassion and power: You have reached out to us through your Beloved Child, Jesus. Grant us courage and faith to serve you by reaching out to others in healing and hope, through Christ our Saviour; to whom with you and the Spirit, one holy God, be honour and praise, now and forever.

Maggie Muldoon-Burr, 1991

God of refreshment: Call us from the concerns of our daily lives to be nourished anew by your presence, that we may live faithfully as sisters and brothers in your church and as servants in your world. May our service drive us to worship and our worship empower us for service; through Christ, our Risen Saviour.

Lynette Miller, 1983

Calls to Worship

In the Reformation Church, the rather stark "Let us worship God..." tended to replace the ancient Apostolic Greeting. This was called "Prefacing." In the nineteenth century, the Preface was often amplified by the addition of a verse from scripture: "The earth is the Lord's and the fullness thereof, the world and they that dwell therein. Let us worship God." Since the 1960s, more contemporary "Calls to Worship" have become common. Sometimes they are printed and said responsively.

1. Christ be with you.
2. And also with you.
1. God's Spirit calls to our spirits,
2. inviting us to worship.
1. God's Spirit calls to our spirits,
2. luring us by love.
1. God's Spirit calls to our spirits,
2. calling us by name, calling us to grow in faith, calling us to be made new.
1. Let us worship God.

Paul Fayter, 1991

1. In the beginning was God. God's Spirit moved across space and time. From chaos was order established; from darkness came forth light; from the very stuff of the earth was humanity created. God gave life with the breath of God's Spirit.
2. We rejoice in the life we have been given. We come to worship God our Creator. Thanks be to God!

Pat Milliken, 1991

1. In the name of God,
2. wondrous, mysterious, marvellous.
1. In the name of Jesus,
2. among us, beyond us, with us.
1. In the name of the Spirit,

2. strange, startling, shaking:
1. I call you to worship.
2. We come to lift our hearts and minds, to open our lips and our lives, to celebrate our God.
1. God calls us to God's way in our time.
2. We accept that call!

St. Stephen's-Broadway, Winnipeg, Man., 1977

May our hearts be in tune with God's Spirit, may our minds think God's thoughts, and may we share our songs of praise with all the world—beginning with each other. Come, let us worship.

Stan Errett, 1984

God calls, and we respond; God uplifts, and we are encouraged; God supports, and we are thankful. Come, let us worship God.

Bill Steadman, 1986

1. We come to worship God our Creator,
2. the One who is the source of life.
1. We gather to praise Christ our Liberator,
2. who sets the captives free and has defeated the powers of evil.
1. We worship through the power of the Spirit,
2. God-with-us always, our energizer and guide.
1. In the name of the God who is Three-in-One, we come in worship.

Laura Jo Bell, 1986

We are not here because we have found God, but because God has found us. God has called us to accept the cost and discover the joy of discipleship. God's promise is of forgiveness of sin and fullness of grace, courage to work for justice in the face of evil, power to make peace, hope against hope that God's purposes will be fulfilled.

Blessing and honour, glory and power, be unto God, now and forever.

Paul Fayter, 1987

1. The beauty of the world has been created by God, the joys of the world have been blessed by God, the anger of the world has been heard by God, the fears of the world have been overcome by God.
2. Come, let us worship God.

Laura J. Turnbull, 1988

Come, let us encounter anew the God who moves among us—the God who meets us in praise and song, in forgiveness and new beginnings, in scripture and sermon, in prayer and in offering, in Christian community and in going forth in love. We gather together to worship God.

Terry Shillington, 1990

1. In the presence of the God whose word called the stars into being,
2. we stand in awe.
1. In the presence of the Christ whose arms held little children and whose eyes sparkled with laughter,
2. we stand in trust.
1. In the presence of the Spirit who stirs within us and causes our hearts to thirst for meaning,
2. we stand in longing.
1. Before you, God, giver of life, in search of love and truth and wholeness,
2. we come in worship.

Pat Milliken, 1990

1. Offer your lives to the living God. Sing praise to your Creator and let shouts of joy resound. Celebrate the presence of God in our midst.
2. We have come to celebrate life in the midst of God's world. We respond, with commitment and faith, to the God who is always with us.

Bill Steadman, 1990

Love! The gospel in one word is Love! For God so loved the world that God gave Jesus. It is this God of love we celebrate in worship now.

Heather McLean, 1992

1. Sing to God.
2. Make music that sounds glad celebration.
1. Sing to God.
2. Lift your voices to proclaim wonder, awe, and joy.
1. Sing to God.
2. In melodies of praise and harmonies of thanksgiving.
1. May our lives be hymns of gratitude and songs of faithfulness.
2. We sing to God.

Ted Dodd, 1992

Call to Worship/Prayer of Approach

1. This is the day you have made, O God, and we are the people you have made to live in it.
2. But in order to live, we must worship.
1. We come to celebrate where your Word touches our lives.
2. We come in confession and praise,
1. To hear your Word and share our concerns,
2. To rededicate ourselves and receive strength and nourishment to go forth and live the life you give.
1. We come in the name of Jesus Christ.
2. We welcome Christ's presence with joy.

Beaverlodge United, Beaverlodge, Alta., 1977

Prayers of Approach

The Prayer of Approach differs from the Prayer of the Day only in that its form tends to be a bit freer and that it is sometimes printed in the order of worship and said in unison. Again, the focus is on God, God's action and God's praise.

Gracious God, on this day of Pentecost we celebrate the coming of your Spirit in power upon your church. We praise you that in all times and places your Spirit has moved in and among your people, bringing energy, purpose, and joy. Send your Spirit upon us today, that we might truly be your people, sent forth in service to the world.

Doreen Van Camp, 1990

Spirit of the Living God, who gathers the church into one body, we gather again in Christ's name to worship you. Make us aware of your presence in what we say and do and dream. Strengthen the ties of faith and affection that bind us together as your people. Strengthen us for love and service in the world ... for Jesus' sake.

Paul Fayter, 1991

Most Holy God, we await the touch of your Spirit this morning. Enter our lives—refreshing, renewing, healing us and our world with the power of your love. So may we love with purpose, enthusiasm, and courage in return, after the manner of Jesus, our Saviour and Friend.

Paul Fayter, 1989

God of grace and mercy: Our restless spirits yearn for your Spirit, our best impulses are founded in your goodness, our faint praises echo the song of creation, our frail lives find life in your beloved Son.

Send your Holy Spirit upon us, that your goodness may flow through us, that our living may be faithful to your will and your way, and that our songs of praise may be heard before your throne of grace.

Lynette Miller, 1986

God, whose creative will is still at work in our world: Bless us this day with your presence and the sense of your purpose. Let the freshening breeze of your Spirit stir and strengthen us. Let us find you again as the shadow of a mighty rock within a weary land. May the everflowing stream of your justice and love cool our fevered rush for self and things; through Christ our Saviour.

Peter Wyatt, 1989

Most Holy God: We rejoice in our awareness of your presence. Enter our lives, refreshing and renewing us through the touch of your Holy Spirit. Grant that we may live with love after the example of Jesus Christ, through whom we pray.

Pat Milliken, 1989

O God, it is exciting to be living through these summer days—times of work and of holiday, times to be with family and friends, time to travel and experience new things, time to play and time to be re-created.

We recognize with gratitude that, though so much of our lives seems to be ruled by forces beyond our control, though inflation continues, though economic injustice grows, though violence, tension, and terror remain very much a part of our world, yet the seasons continue their cycle, crops ripen and gardens grow, babies are born and people laugh and love and enjoy each other.

We come in the faith that love and life defeat hatred and death. It is still your world, and we live in it in joy.

Beaverlodge United, Beaverlodge, Alta., 1978

Gracious God we come in worship, proclaiming that we recognize your gift of life and are grateful for it. Our living is not easy; it is not easy to live well. So we look to you to lead us onward, through the joy and hurt, the confusion and love, which awaits each and all of us. Lead us into newness of life, we pray.

Harold Wells, 1984

Be with us, God, as we gather in worship. Renew us as we face the challenge of this day. Give us the strength to be a committed people. You call us to serve and to share as citizens of your coming community. We ask your blessing on our commitment; in the name of Jesus the Christ.

Bill Steadman, 1988

Gracious and loving God, we come seeking your presence in worship. Through our songs of praise we seek you; by our words of prayer we reach out to you. Grant that we may hear your voice and not merely echoes of our own. Fill us with your Spirit; bless us by your grace; surround us with your love, now and always.

Pat Milliken, 1990

Giving and loving God, we are people who hunger for your truth. May this time of worship so nourish and strengthen us that we will serve with renewed confidence. Fill our hearts with joy and love. This we pray in the name of the One who fed the multitudes and ministered to the needy.

Laura J. Turnbull, 1990

1. Touch us, loving God, with the joy of your presence. Touch us and hold us.
LEFT: The misty lake and rocky shore, the green of leaf and gold of field, tell of your creative presence.

RIGHT: The comfort of experiences shared, the sense of deepening trust in one another, tell of your supportive presence.
LEFT: Our knowledge of hurting persons healed, of the powerless dignified, tells of your compassionate presence.
RIGHT: Our anxiety lessened, our fears put to rest, tells of your peaceful presence.
ALL: Jesus, one-with-us, reassure us of your loving presence. Touch us and hold us, ever-present God, and never let us go.

The Community Church, Terrace Bay, Ont., 1990

Lord of life and love and healing laughter: We come again today to the place where we have seen your smiling face, felt the warmth of your friendship, the support of your everlasting arms. We come to renew our covenant with you. Be with us, God, as we delight in your goodness and are strengthened to follow in your way.

Marjorie Bradley, 1990

O God, you have called us together to worship just as we are. We cannot pretend to be what we are not, for you have made us and know us through and through. In our weakness we come with prayers for strength; in our strength we come with prayers of thanksgiving. Open our hearts that we might pray with honesty and await your answers with renewed faith. Let our praise and our worship be unrestrained.

Dawn Ballantine-Dickson, 1990

Gracious God, you have called us to be your own. We long to respond to your call: openly, fully, lovingly. Hear our deepest desires and yearnings we pray. Reveal yourself in Spirit and in truth.

Olga McKellar, 1990

Out of earth's dust you have breathed us into life, O God. You have made us and we are yours. Enable us in this worship to sense your strong presence and accept with humility your gentle guidance in all our living.

Jack Ballantine-Dickson, 1990

God of creation, giver of joy, on the Sabbath you sat down to rest. Around you was all creation: stars danced across the heavens, the wind wove melodies through the trees, men and women walked together and knew joy. You looked and saw that it was good.

On this summer Sunday, may we simply sit and rest. May we sense your creation all around us, and see that it is good. Show us how to walk softly on the earth, and together in love.

Pat Milliken, 1991

O God, potter of our humanity: Turn us, form us, shape us with the creative finger of your eternal love.

Peter Wyatt, 1992

Prayers of Confession

A useful format for confession is that of: General Confession *(printed, said in unison or responsively);* silent prayer; a sung response such as the Kyrie Eleison or Agnus Dei; Assurance of Forgiveness; Hymn of Praise or Doxology *(all standing).* This moves us from general confession, through personal confession, to the assurance of God's grace to which we respond with a burst of praise. The action of standing for praise is an important embodiment of being a forgiven people. (And perhaps we should capture again the tradition of kneeling for confession?)

God of windy breath, blow into our lives; God of fiery presence, burn away our despair. We bear in our lives the world's dis-ease: prejudice, selfishness, anger, fear. We are burdened with our incompleteness; broken and shrivelled up we have lost hope.

Touch us with your Spirit, God. Moisten the dry places with tears of love; mend the broken places with bonds of hope. Birth us as your new creations, that we might come alive in the Spirit's power.

Jack Ballantine-Dickson, 1990

O God, we confess that we are forever confessing, forever counting on your promise of forgiveness but not on the life-renewing power of your Spirit. Let that Spirit move among us now; let it burn away all conceit and self-love, all laziness and sloth. Let it move and transform us before we confess again.

John McTavish, 1976

O God from whom all blessings flow: Lead us by the inspiration of your Holy Spirit to think those things which are right, and enable us by the power of your love to do them.

We confess the ease with which we hurt one another; the ease with which we turn our backs on the hurt of the world. We confess that so often we seek our own security over the common good. Enable us to feel and know true sisterly/brotherly care within one family. Encourage us to be the community of your people, the Body of Christ in the world.

Kenneth Wotherspoon, 1984

O God, whose Spirit came in tongues of fire, save us from the fire of our tongues. Forgive us the sharp comment, the unkind cut, the easy lie, the smooth flattery. And pardon our silences: the witness not made, the truth unspoken, the comfort held back, the praise not offered. By your living Word, empower our words, that in the freedom of forgiveness we may serve you in joy... *(silent prayer)*

Lord, have mercy. Christ, have mercy. Lord, have mercy.

Lynette Miller, 1985

We confess, O God, that by silence or an ill-chosen word we have constructed walls of prejudice; that by selfishness and lack of simple sympathy we have refused to give ourselves away; that in concern for our own safety and the security of our reputations we have passed by on the other side; that by obsession with our own affairs we have had no time for others. In your mercy, accept, redeem, empower us, O God, we pray.

Harold Boyd, 1980

Break up the hard-packed soil of our nation, God, and let there be shoots of new life. Deliver us from narrow ways that speak of "we" and "they," that rest upon ignorance or apathy. Deliver us from silence when faithful people must speak out, when old truths need repeating and division may be bridged by insight. Deliver us from the noise of too much busyness with too little purpose, from pleasure seeking that is self-centred rather than renewing, from wealth while much of the world is impoverished. Prepare us for the peace that grows out of reconciliation, for the change that matters and is constructive, and for the service that binds us into human community.

Terry Shillington, 1982

We confess, O God, that we have not lived up to the high calling of Christian service. Where we have turned away from others' need, where we have refused to respond to others' hurt, where we have failed to proclaim your good news: Good God, forgive us.... *(silent confession)*

1. Lord, have mercy. 2. Christ, have mercy.
1. Lord, have mercy.

Gordon Churchill, 1988

Loving, Creator God: We examine our lives in confession this morning, not in an attitude of fear, for when we confess our unfaithfulness we are assured of your faithful love. And when we look at our lives, our church, our world, and see so much that falls short of fullness, we would be overwhelmed by despair except for your overwhelming care.

Grant us the making-new power of forgiveness that we might begin afresh, this time with our hands more firmly clasped in yours.

Thomas Harding, 1990

Compassionate and liberating God, week after week we acknowledge our sins only to turn again and continue in past patterns. Free us from that which restricts new life. We admit that discouragement, despair and uncertainty have blocked us from embracing a new vision. Open our eyes to wonder and our lives to accept your way of love and peace.

Laura J. Turnbull, 1990

In confession, O God, we acknowledge our failure: We have failed to hear your Word and have heeded, instead, the world's words; we have failed to seek your light and have sought, instead, lesser lights; we have been forgetful of your will and have followed, instead, our own whims, wishes, and wonderings. But we long, O God, for your empowering love.

Have compassion on our failure. Lift from us the mantle of despair, and free us to live in fullness as your children.

Pat Milliken, 1991

In this season of summer let us make our confession.

In this season of warmth, O God, we confess those times when we have been cool in relationships and distant in friendships... *(silence)*

In this season of relaxation we confess those times when we have not let go of attitudes that cut others off and have not kept to ourselves words that wound... *(silence)*

In this season of plenty we confess those times when we have hoarded your gifts and turned away from those desperate for bare necessities... *(silence)*

In this season of growth, O God, coax us into newness, into wholeness, into life.

David Sparks, 1990

O God the gardener, in straw hat and worn white gloves you set to work: digging, weeding, watering. How joyful you are in your work. You do not force the growth. You breathe upon the soil, dropping your sweat upon its waiting clumps—and by unseen grace the garden grows.

We kneel beside you, seeking our work in yours. Bid us dig into our relationships, loving with healing love, living with healing intent. Bid us weed our thoughts, pulling out those of little value. Spacing and pruning the gems of wisdom, bid us water our hopes—pressing for a crop beyond our right.

Forgive us our laziness and grant us redeeming sweat. Forgive us our guilt and grant us grace for growing.

O God the gardener, grow in us—that we might labour till the crops be ripe and whole.

G. Malcolm Sinclair, 1991

O God, who is life and hope and newness: We confess that it is easier to be lazy than to be lively; that it is more comfortable to take our ease than to be on the growing edge; that it is safer to make rules than to wrestle with the complexity of relationships. Be gentle with us, yet firm. Be gracious toward our failings, yet unrelenting in your call to wholeness. This we pray through the One who accepts, forgives, and challenges us into life in all its wholeness.

Gordon Churchill, 1992

Assurances of Pardon/Forgiveness

Sometimes Assurances of Forgiveness are presented in a conditional manner: *If* we do such and such ... *then* God forgives. Many have found, however, that a *declarative* Assurance ("We *are* a forgiven people...") is both theologically and psychologically stronger.

1. The Risen Christ appeared to the disciples and breathed on them, saying: "Peace be with you. Receive the Holy Spirit. Your sins are forgiven."
2. Our sins are forgiven. We forgive one another. Thanks be to God we are free!

Arlene Caswell/John Mastandrea, 1991

Sisters and brothers, know that God is rich in mercy and abundant in compassion. Even though we are bound by sin and the failures of the past, God's great love for us breathes us into life through Jesus Christ our Saviour and in the power of the Holy Spirit.

We are a forgiven people. Thanks be to God!

Paul Fayter, 1986

The God of abundant love and amazing grace reaches out to us in Christ Jesus. Admitting those times we have fallen short and missed the mark, we are open to the healing love of God and the forgiveness and freedom of life in the Spirit. We are a forgiven people. Come alive in Christ!

Paul Fayter, 1987

The psalmist cried: "Create in me a clean heart, O God, and renew a right spirit within me." Be assured, sisters and brothers, that God's Spirit wrestles within us to bring healing to our spirits and the determination to live in newness to our hearts.

We are accepted, forgiven, and empowered into newness. Thanks be to God.

Gordon Churchill, 1988

God is compassion, forgiveness, transforming power. God's unfailing love sustains and upholds us. God will never let us go. Where the Spirit is, there is freedom. Receive God's forgiveness. Come alive in Christ!

Jane V. Doull, 1990

There is no sin so terrible that God cannot forgive, no hurt so terrible that God cannot heal. God accepts, God forgives, God sets free. Receive the forgiving love of God.

Don Daniels, 1978

1. This is good news if we will but listen: God loves us, God forgives us, God accepts us and sets us free. In the name of Christ we are forgiven!
2. In the name of Christ we are forgiven! Thanks to God!

Beaverlodge United, Beaverlodge, Alta., 1978

No matter where we are, God is there.
No matter what we have done, God forgives.
No matter our reluctance to accept God, God has accepted us.
With that assurance, receive forgiveness and live in fullness and in hope.

Bill Steadman, 1986

1. Through the generosity and love of God we are forgiven. This is good news!
2. To the One who loves us and has freed us from our sins be glory and dominion forever and ever. Amen. (Rev. 1:5b-6)

Laura J. Turnbull, 1990

1. Sisters and brothers, God transforms our weakness and brokenness into strengthened faith and renewed hope. God empowers us to do more than we can imagine to be possible. Accept the forgiving love of God.
2. We accept God's forgiveness. Thanks be to God!

Jane V. Doull, 1990

Hear the words of the Apostle Paul who assures us of God's forgiveness: "Grace to you and peace from God, and from our Saviour Jesus Christ, whom God has raised from the dead and who delivers us from evil, according to God's gracious will. To God be the glory, forever and ever."

Paul Fayter, 1991

God's love is like gentle rain on a hot summer's day. It is love that accepts, forgives, and frees us to begin life anew. We are a forgiven people. Thanks be to God!

Laura J. Turnbull, 1991

A major difference between the 1969 *Service Book* order and the 1984 *Sunday Liturgy* pattern is in the placing of the offering and prayers. The *Service Book* suggests: Hymn of Response, Offering and Prayer of Dedication, Announcements, Prayers of Thanksgiving and Intercession concluding with the Lord's Prayer. The *Sunday Liturgy,* in order to cluster those elements of the service which centre around the Table, suggests: Hymn of Response, Announcements, Prayers of the People (intercessions only) as part of the Service of the Word; and then, moving to the Service of the Table: the Peace, Offering, Prayers of Thanksgiving and Dedication concluding with the Lord's Prayer.

In the prayers which follow, the Offertory Prayers and Prayers of Thanksgiving and Intercession are according to the *Service Book* format; the Prayers of the People and Prayers of Thanksgiving and Dedication are according to the *Sunday Liturgy* pattern.

Offertory Prayers

Good and giving God, we thank you for the privilege not only of receiving your gifts, but also for the privilege of *being* your gifts—to each other and to the world. Receive our offering, we pray. Through it and through us, bless your world.

Christopher McKibbon, 1981

Bringer-to-birth, receive all we offer you this day. May your Holy Spirit maintain the labour of creation through the lives of your faithful ones; through Jesus Christ.

Arlene Caswell/John Mastandrea, 1991

O God, who once fed the multitude with a handful of loaves and fishes: May our little, offered to you, become an abundance. Increase our hearts' desire to give gladly of our best. Through Christ we pray.

Peter Wyatt, 1988

We are grateful, God, that your Spirit is at work within us, nudging and stretching us, causing us to grow in understanding and service. May these offerings be an expression of our gratitude for all your gifts; and may our lives be an expression of your love for the world.

Hilbert Berger, 1986

With this offering we present also ourselves, O God: our joy and our tears, our laughter and our loneliness, our sorrow for past mistakes and our resolve for a better future. Accept us in our offering we pray, for Jesus' sake.

Peter Wyatt, 1988

O God, before whose face only the truth of compassion can finally stand: Accept our offering as a gift of thanksgiving. May it be money of mercy in this world of pain and despair. Use it to declare the healing power and wondrous hope of your love in Christ Jesus.

Peter Wyatt, 1988

Because of your great love for us, O God, we express our love for your church and for others through the bringing of these gifts. Accept them, please. Enable us to use them in Christ's name.

Thomas Harding, 1990

Faithful God of justice: Here is the work of our hands; here is the love of our hearts. Bless these gifts and grant us spirits of generosity, joy, and thanksgiving as we seek to do your will in the world.

Paul Fayter, 1991

O God, who gave us Jesus as the bread of life: We respond by offering ourselves as dough to be made alive by the gospel's leaven. Knead us and shape us to suit your will. Flavour us with the richness of Christ's teachings. Enable us to rise in the power of the Spirit, that we might go forth from our worship as bread for the world.

Dawn Ballantine-Dickson, 1990

Prayers of Thanksgiving and Intercession

All praise and honour, glory and thanksgiving be unto you, Creator God. In the beginning your Spirit brooded over the waters; and when you formed us from the dust of the earth you breathed into us the breath of life. Even when we resisted your mercy, fell into unfaithfulness and grieved you, O God, your Spirit came upon the prophets, empowering them to speak your word of holy judgement and steadfast love.

In the fullness of time you gave your Child, Jesus, to be for us the Way, the Truth, and the Life. At his baptism your Spirit descended like a dove and named him "Beloved." Filled with your Spirit he proclaimed good news to the poor, release to the captives, sight for the blind, liberty for the oppressed. In the power of your Spirit he confronted the powers of sin and death and died, for us and all creation, upon the cross. But you raised him from death, and he has promised to be with us, even to the end of everything. So he will come again in glory, to bring into being the consummation of the ages.

Send your Spirit, God, on us, as on the day of Pentecost. Like a mighty, rushing wind, blow through the hollow spaces of our lives, bringing new life, and power, and unity. With dancing tongues of holy fire set our hearts aflame with love for you and all you love. Come, Holy Spirit, come.

Remember, God, the people of your church. Heal our brokenness. Preserve our going out and our coming in. Gather us together as one body, sign of your new and eternal community. By the baptism of water and Spirit, scatter us abroad as seeds on the wind, to be your witnesses to the world.

Most wise and mighty God, we your sons and daughters pray for the gifts of your Spirit: knowledge and joy, peace and patience, humility and hope, faith and love, kindness and compassion. Seek and sustain our souls. Save us and sanctify us, for we move in fear and frustration through a world of violence, indifference, and injustice. Let your Spirit groan with our spirits as we await the dawning of your final glory. In all things, guide, support, and empower us, God we pray.

Paul Fayter, 1986

We ask for the ear, O God, that discerns your voice amidst the babble of our days. Long the tongues which distract and divide have held captive our hearing; long the language of dominance and disrespect has passed for speech among us; long have we listened to vain voices promising quick fixes and ready prosperity, counselling us to compromise, to take the easy way. Long, too, have we contributed to the confusion of tongues our own false song, preaching an acceptable gospel and fearing to sing the Lord's song in a strange land.

All this we acknowledge; all this we confess—the consequences of our frail efforts to scale the heavens and overpower the High and Holy One.

O you who scatters us as we build proud towers that cannot reach heaven, temper our hearing that it might yet resonate with your Word in the lands of our dispersion. And in our separateness, may yet there be found a common tongue of praise.

Teach us, as at Pentecost, that we need not sing a single melody in order to be of one voice. Draw us into that gifted and loved community which does not require sameness, but which has respect for the songs of those who are faithfully different. And grant that our life together in the Spirit may be modelled after that surprising Kingdom in which there is no babbling, nor any silence, but one eternal music.

Donald R. Ross, 1992

1. God of the greening leaf and bursting flower, we praise you in the midst of your wonder-filled creation. We thank you for the love that guides us into learning and growth... *(silence)*
   God of leaf and flower, 2. Clear our eyes to see your vision.

1. God of the broken branch and ravaged forest, we pray for those who are denied opportunities for growth—the exploited, those marginalized because of colour, sex, nationality, class, age... *(silence)*
   God of branch and forest, 2. Clear our minds to know your vision.

1. God of withered shoot and blighted grain, we pray for those whose growth can only be found in the search for healing—physically, emotionally, spiritually... *(silence)*
   God of shoot and grain, 2. Clear our spirits to trust your vision.

1. God of the trailing vine and firm root, we pray for ourselves as we seek to grow in our response to your call to mission in the world... *(silence)*
   God of vine and root, 2. Clear our hearts to live your vision; in Jesus' name we pray.

Caryn Douglas, 1990

O Great Spirit, whose voice we hear on the wind, whose breath gives life to the world, hear us. We come to you as but a few of your many children. We are small and weak. We need your strength and wisdom.

May we walk in beauty. May our eyes ever behold the red and purple sunset. May our hands respect the things that you have made and our ears be sharp to hear your voice.

Make us wise that we may know the things that you have taught your children, the lessons hidden in every leaf and rock. Make us strong, not to be superior to our sisters and brothers, but to be able to fight our greatest enemy—ourselves. Make us ever ready to come to you with straight eyes so that, when our lives fade, as the fading sunset, our spirits will come to you without shame.

Traditional, S/A, 1990

Hot rooms, hot tempers, the heat of accusation and counter-accusation in the courts and councils, the bargaining sessions and assemblies of our city, nation, and world. You, God, are the cooling presence—the voice of quiet, reasonable men and women, the way of saving face, the affirmation that all can be winners. Cool us down, O God!

Fiery words, hasty judgements, insults hurled back and forth—families in conflict, misunderstanding between friend and friend, worker and boss, parent and child. You, God, are the reconciling presence—building bridges, restoring communication, searching for common ground. Create again community, O God.

Fevers rising, illness dragging on, emotions shattered by death, decision-making difficult, stress too much to bear. You, God, are the hopeful presence—the hand of the sensitive nurse, the human hug, the whispered word of comfort, the sign of possibility. Be dawn in our darkness, O God.

In the heat of summer, breathe your cool breeze; in the desert of our frustration, pour out your cool water. Refresh, renew, rejuvenate, O God, our healer and our hope.

David Sparks, 1990

Creating and sanctifying God, we praise and bless you for all your good gifts: for love and friendship and laughter, for times and places of re-creation, for the people of this faith community, for those fired with a vision of your just and peaceful reign in a world too often cruel and hurtful. We thank you especially for Jesus, the shepherd and saviour of our souls, who is eternally alive with you, who lives and moves among us now, leading us to the fullness of life that goes on forever.

God, we are poor in spirit; and though we often pretend that we can make it on our own, we need you so. We lift to you our need, and the needs of all the world, groaning in travail. We need your surrounding love. We need you here beside us to lift us when we fall. We need you behind us, prodding and provoking. We need you ahead of us, guiding us on our way. Challenge and encourage us when we are weak and weary.

We pray for sisters and brothers whom we know, and for all in need, known only to you....

God, though we are poor in spirit, we are blessed. For we know our poverty and trust in the riches of your grace, poured out upon us and upon the whole creation. In the name of the One who is risen, and reigns, we pray in the ancient words: Our Father....

Paul Fayter, 1991

1. O God, help us to know you as the Creative One who joins together the smallest blade of grass and the farthest star, as the Love which is so great that it leans down from heaven to aid us in our every action.

2. We are your children: never forgotten, never deserted, always forgiven, always loved.

1. O God, help us to know you as the One who was there at our beginning and will be at our ending, the One who calls us now and will continue to call through whatever may happen in our lives.
2. We are your children: never forgotten....

1. O God, take us by the hand; forgive us when we fail; lift us when we fall; enable us to try again.
2. Mother/Father strengthen us; faithful Christ walk with us; Holy Spirit lead us; for we are your children: never forgotten, never deserted, always forgiven, always loved.

John Haynes, 1992

A Prayer for All Who Dance

O God of dance, who flung the sun and stars into their places and moved among all the creatures of your creation: Come to us as we offer to you our prayers for all who dance.

We pray with those who dance with the burden of hunger, starvation, and emptiness heavy in their gut;

we pray with those who dance in fear and worry, frustration and despair;

we pray with those who must dance upon the broken glass of injustice and the hot coals of revenge;

we pray with the lost who don't know where to dance, with the lonely who have no one to dance with, with the disenfranchised whose choice of dance is taken from them, with the powerless who can no longer dance;

and we pray with those who dance with great joy and firm hope, infectious purpose and sacrificial love, and with a sparkle in their eyes.

Lord of the dance, we all dance together in the great liturgy of life in our own time and place. Fill us with your Spirit, that we might live and move and have our being in the newness and fullness of Christ.

David Spence, 1977

Prayers of the People

> The Prayers of the People are intended to be just that: the prayers of the *people!* These could be written and led by a lay person, perhaps offered from a microphone situated half way down the centre aisle (symbolizing that the prayers come from the *midst* of the people). If led by the worship leader, the prayers need to have spaces in them for people to do their own praying.

Energizing God, we look at your world and the future seems so bleak: assassinations, the will to war, inequalities, the potential for disaster—all seem so overwhelming... *(silent prayer)*. And then your Spirit comes—gently comes, earnestly comes—reminding us of communities which are at peace, telling of times of reconciliation, pointing to areas of hope.

When we consider the needs of those around us, the problems seem so immense: church members in hospital, families in conflict, friends who mourn the death of one they have loved... *(silent prayer)*. And then your Spirit comes—gently comes, calmly comes—suggesting what we might do to help, strengthening the faith of those who are afraid, bringing courage and hope where there was none before.

When we think of the needs of our church, the range is so vast: the need for caring in our community, the call to action for those who need daycare, the sense of responsibility for mission both at home and overseas... *(silent prayer)*. And then your Spirit comes—gently comes, persistently comes—issuing us a challenge, enabling us to search for options, stirring us to action, calling us to be people of vision.

When we consider ourselves, we see how far we fall short of faithful living: stymied by tough decisions, confused in our values, secretly worried about our health or our financial future... *(silent prayer)*. And then your Spirit comes—gently comes, reassuringly comes—to give us new confidence, to slow us down, to show what scope there is for our special gifts and capabilities.

(Silent prayer) Gentle, effective Spirit: come gently, come effectively, today!

David Sparks, 1990

1. That you will be among us, that we might be your people, remembering who we are:
   Knowing you will answer, 2. We pray to you, O God.

1. For those making decisions in the councils of the nations, that they may act in accordance with your will and keep alive the possibility of justice and shalom:
   Knowing you will answer, 2. We pray to you, O God.

1. For Christ's church universal, and for all faith communities, that we may grow in unity and service, doing your will:
   Knowing you will answer...

1. For this congregation: for our particular concerns—as families, as single people, that we might see your hand in our affairs:
   Knowing you will answer...

1. We cry out with those who are hungry, those who are oppressed. We pray for the courage to act in your freedom.
   Knowing you will answer...

1. We pray with those who are ill, especially those we name, silently or aloud ... with those in prison, the lonely, and all in situations difficult to bear:
   Knowing you will answer...

1. We pray for the departed, especially those we hold before you....
   Knowing you will answer...

1. As companions of the One who is the Prince of

Peace, we pray for peace in our hearts, peace in our church, peace in our world.

Knowing you will answer...

Elizabeth Beale, 1987

We join now in prayer as the people of God. Where there are silences, use them to offer your personal prayers.

Gracious God, you have created us; you have set us free and loved us into life; you have spoken your word and shown us your way. Acknowledging that you will have your way with us, we bring our prayers for this day.

For the Church of Jesus Christ around the world, and especially for our sisters and brothers who are being tested for the faith and for what they believe to be right: Hear our prayers, gracious God... *(silence)*

For The United Church of Canada, for our sister churches across this land, and for this congregation, _____, that we might be faithful to our calling: Hear our prayers, gracious God... *(silence)*

For the leaders of the nations and for all in positions of power and responsibility, that justice might be done and that the world might be governed rightly: Hear our prayers, gracious God...

For those we know and name now—for family members, friends, folk of this congregation, neighbours who need our prayers: Hear our prayers, gracious God...

And for ourselves we pray. With your power, God, preserve us; in your wisdom guide us; with your love protect us; in your way direct us. Guard us against the powers of evil and lead us into your coming community.

Christ with us, Christ in us, Christ over us, Christ before us. All glory be to you, sovereign of all.

Thomas Harding, 1990

Prayers of Thanksgiving and Dedication

You have set us in a world of ancient truth, new discovery, and profound mystery, O God. Draw us anew into the excitement of Pentecost. You have gifted us with revelation and tradition; you have rooted us in a family tree rich with the story of strong saints, dramatic sin, and marvellous grace. We are nudged into new life by the provocation of your Holy Spirit, energized to be your people.

Thankful to be part of that tree of faith we offer our gifts, praying that through what we offer your church may seek ever deeper roots for times of trouble and trial. And we offer ourselves as your witnesses, seeking to be open to the breath of your Spirit, seeking a renewed faith that dances like flames of fire, radiates your gentle tenderness, and speaks in tongues of excitement and hope.

Terry Shillington, 1988

Gracious God, we praise you for your caring and challenging presence in our midst. We praise and thank you for calling us to be disciples and trusting us to do your work. We thank you for the gifts you have given each of us to enable us to serve you and one another. As we return these gifts to you, may the power of your Holy Spirit inflame us with a desire to share in the work of loving, healing and nourishing all your people today and always. In Jesus' name we pray.

Jane V. Doull, 1990

1. O God, you are gracious and righteous and have filled our hearts with joy. We are thankful for all creation: for the world we live in, for our families and friends, for everything that comes from your bountiful hand.
2. Everything we have comes from you, O God.

1. We are thankful for our human successes: for the goals we have reached, for the determination to set new goals, for your support when our goals seem out of reach.
2. Everything we have comes from you, O God.

1. Above all else we are thankful for your unending love: for your faithfulness to all creation, for the gift of new life through your Holy Spirit, for the gift of yourself in Jesus our Saviour.
2. Everything we have comes from you, O God.

1. Accept now these gifts we bring....

Blaine Gregg, 1987

O God, we thank you for the gift of imagination that enhances our lives and our world with beauty and grace, especially in the grey times, the times of sorrow and loss.

We thank you for the gift of celebration, for the lost and found, for the gone but not forgotten, especially in the slow, sad times when we are sleepless with sorrow.

We thank you for the gift of courage, when we take ourselves in hand and offer ourselves in service to others, especially in the dark and troubled times.

We thank you for the gift of life, and the promise it contains of wider, richer life to come.

And so receive these gifts we bring....

Keith R. Maddock, 1991

A Post-Communion Prayer

We thank you, God, for the gifts you give us: for the bread of our being loved, for the wine of our joy, for our life together as people ready to do the work of love and justice. And now we pray that, having been refreshed at this table, we may be bread and wine for each other and for the world.

barb m. janes, 1992

Commissionings and Benedictions

One of the more brilliant innovations of the 1969 *Service Book* was the addition of a Commissioning before the final Benediction. The Commissioning sends us forth, but it does not take the place of the Benediction (though often the two are combined). People still need to have a sense of God's hand upon them as they go forth from worship.

1. Let us bless God, our Creator.
2. Blessed be God forever.
1. Let us bless Christ, our Saviour.
2. Blessed be Christ forever.
1. Let us bless the Spirit, the Comforter.
2. Blessed be the Spirit forever.
1. May the blessing of Almighty God, Creator, Saviour, and Comforter, be with us all, now and forever.
2. Amen.

Sylvia Dunstan, 1987

May the blessing of God our Creator who formed us from the dust,
and the blessing of Jesus our Redeemer who conquered death with life,
and the blessing of the Spirit who brings to life dry bones:
give life to you, to the church and to the world,
making of us a new creation.

Neil Parker, 1986

Unless the eye catch fire, God will not be seen.
Unless the ear catch fire, God will not be heard.
Unless the tongue catch fire, God will not be named.
Unless the heart catch fire, God will not be loved.
Unless the mind catch fire, God will not be known.

Holy God of justice, living Spirit of power, Jesus Christ our peace, may we burn, body and soul, with love for you, each other, and all creation.

Go forth with the blessing of the God of Pentecost. Go forth surrounded by the Spirit's flaming love.

Paul Fayter, 1987

1. God be with you.
2. And also with you.
1. We go forth to love and serve God and our neighbour,
2. In the name of Christ and through the power of the Holy Spirit.
1. May God's Spirit breathe through us, warming and strengthening us and renewing the whole of creation.
2. To God: Creator, Christ and Spirit, be eternal praise.

Jane V. Doull, 1990

1. As we go from this place into our daily living, our lives will be a testimony to what we have done and been given here. Go to be the people of God.
2. We go to be Christ's Body in the world.
1. Go in joy, in love, and in peace.
2. We go praising God, witnessing to the Risen Christ, empowered by the Holy Spirit.

Don Daniel, 1983

1. As Jesus sent the disciples out into the world to preach and to heal, so Christ sends us to speak words of hope and to heal human hurts today.
2. We accept his mission to be God's people in the world.
1. Go on your way, rejoicing in the presence of the Risen Christ and in the power of the gospel of love and hope.
2. To God be the glory, now and forever. Amen.

Ken Wotherspoon, 1984

1. We are Exodus, moving from slavery into freedom.
2. We are Advent, longing for the fulfilment of creation.
1. We are Christmas, filled with the Christ who is present.
2. We are Epiphany, shining for all to see.
1. We are Lent, journeying to cross and resurrection.
2. We are Easter, rising with the risen Christ.
1. We are Pentecost, bursting with the life of the Spirit.
2. Go to be God's people in the world!

Don Daniel, 1986

1. God has spoken. Now let our living reflect that Word.
2. We go forth to be God's people in the world.

Don Daniel, 1982

Our worship ends and our work begins. Go with the blessing of God.

Don Daniel, 1983

We have sung God's praise with our lips for the meaning and richness life holds for us. We go forth now to live God's praise in our lives, through the Christ who goes before us.

Max Surjadinata, 1985

The blessing of the Holy One of Israel,
the blessing of Jesus Christ the Righteous,
the blessing of our Comfort and Counsellor,
be with you now and forever.
Go into the world, clothed with the glory of Jesus,
walking in the light of Christ.

Sylvia Dunstan, 1987

Go forth remembering whose you are: And the blessing of God, the giver of every good and perfect gift; and of Christ, who summons us to service; and of the Holy Spirit, who breathes generosity and love, be with us all.

Peter Wyatt, 1988

1. The earth is God's and the fullness thereof.
2. The world and all that dwell therein.
1. Creation is groaning, waiting for God's children to be revealed.
2. We go forth to take our place in the birth pangs of God's new age.
1. As we go: May the blessing of God, Creator, Christ and Spirit, go with us all.

Sylvia Dunstan, 1988

Go forth, knowing that—
    the love of God is yours to share,
    the peace of Christ is yours to impart,
    the power of the Holy Spirit is yours to enable.

Audrey Lans, 1990

Chapter
Two

The Autumn

Prayers for Anniversary Sunday   69

Prayers for Worldwide Communion Sunday   71

Prayers for Thanksgiving Sunday   72

Prayers for Stewardship Sunday   74

Prayers for All Saints' Sunday   75

Prayers for Peace Sabbath/Remembrance Day   77

Prayers for the Sovereignty of Christ Sunday   81

A Prayer for Late Evening Worship   82

CIVIL CALENDAR AND CHRISTIAN CALENDAR

How is it, we are sometimes asked, that there are so few resources in *Gathering* for such civil holidays as Canada Day, Labour Day, or Remembrance Day? Have we forgotten that the real world out there exists?

A question that persistently confronts the planners of worship is how to observe such "high" days in the civil calendar. Thanksgiving Day, while also a civil holiday, presents no problem since worship on *any* Sunday is thanksgiving—indeed, is intended to be "eucharistic," which means thankful. But what about those other days?

On the one hand, we cannot ignore the world's agenda and still be faithful to a very worldly God. To pretend that November 11 is just another day and not one of deep significance in the hearts and minds of many people would be pastorally irresponsible. And perhaps we would be missing a prophetic opportunity to address the issues of war and peace.

On the other hand, the point of using the lectionary is to affirm that the church lives not by the civil calendar but by the rhythm of the Christian year which annually remembers the events, great and small, in the story of salvation. As a faith community we have a unique agenda. It takes priority over the world's agenda in the shaping of our corporate worship.

What, then, are we to do in our churches about Canada Day, Labour Day, Remembrance Day—or, more specifically, the Sundays nearest to them?

We might think that they are too insignificant to do *anything* with. Or, we might scrap the lectionary and rummage through the scripture for passages that seem to "fit." Or, we might ask the question: What has the Word to say to us and to our society on this special occasion? And, with that question in mind, listen again to the lessons that happen to be prescribed for the day.

There is no ironclad guarantee that there will be any "word from the Lord." But it is surprising, and often exhilarating, to discover that there is a word for the occasion in one or other of the day's lessons. It's a word we might not have heard had we gone the "rummaging" route.

It's all a matter of priorities. It's a question of a starting point, or of what drum we are marching to.

The acid test of our priorities will come in that spring when, lo, Mother's Day (or, if you like, Christian Family Sunday) and Pentecost fall on the same day! Some will simply ignore Mother's Day. Some will simply ignore Pentecost. Some might discover a Pentecostal word for the church on Mother's Day.

Meanwhile, during this "Ordinary Time," pray and preach and celebrate well as the story unfolds to address the very real world in which we live.

Fred McNally, 1987

IDEAS AND RESOURCES FOR THE AUTUMN

A Litany for the Commissioning of Church School Teachers

LEADER: "Hear O Israel, God alone is God. Love the Lord your God with all your heart, and soul, and mind and strength. Never forget these commands I give you today, and teach them to your children" (Deut. 6:4-7).

ADULTS: We rejoice in the faith which has been handed on to us. This faith we desire to hand on to our children.

YOUNG PEOPLE: We are glad to be part of this family of faith. We want to keep learning God's way.

TEACHERS: And so do we. That is why we teach. We offer ourselves to God and to this congregation, to be used in the ministry of teaching in the Church of Jesus Christ.

ADULTS: We praise God for your commitment. We pledge to you our support in prayer and in action. The teaching you do is on behalf of us all.

YOUNG PEOPLE: We praise God for you also, for your time and your patience and love.

LEADER: Let us pray—
And now, O God, we commission these people who have committed themselves to the ministry of teaching on our behalf. We ask for them strength, creativity, and joy. Touch each of them with your love. Enable them to feel our support and love as they do this important work. In the name of our Saviour Christ we ask this, and for the furtherance of your coming community among us.

N. Macintosh/B. Brazier, 1985

A Covenant Service for the Installation of Teachers in a Church School

A large banner was constructed depicting the United Church crest, with detachable symbols (using Velcro). The banner was draped over a flip chart at the front of the sanctuary with the participants gathered around it, the teachers in a group to one side.

MINISTER: You have accepted a great responsibility in attending to the instruction and guidance of children within our church school. I ask you, then, in the presence of God and of this congregation: Do you believe in God, Creator, Christ and Holy Spirit?

TEACHERS: We do.

MINISTER: Do you promise to be diligent in your preparation and faithful in your witness that the children of our congregation may be enabled to grow in the faith?

TEACHERS: We do.

SUPERINTENDENT: *(placing the dove on the crest)* On behalf of these teachers I place this dove on our crest as a symbol of our dependence on the guidance of the Holy Spirit in our teaching and living.

CHILD: *(placing the open Bible on the crest)* On behalf of these students I place this open Bible on our crest as a symbol of the source of truth and the stories of our faith.

PARENT: *(placing the alpha and omega on the crest)* On behalf of the parents I place this alpha and omega on our crest as a symbol of the living Christ who is the beginning and end of our faith journey.

PARENTS: *(stand and say together)* We welcome you as the teachers of our children. We pledge to you our prayers and support by encouraging our children and talking with them about their lessons, and by providing Christian homes in which they may learn both by word and example.

MEMBER OF CONGREGATION: *(placing the burning bush on the crest)* On behalf of the congregation I place this burning bush on our crest as a symbol of God's indestructible church, of which we are called to be a part and within which we are sisters and brothers together.

ALL COVENANT TOGETHER: In the presence of God and dependent on God's guidance, we covenant together to endeavour to make _____ United Church School a place where the knowledge of Christ will grow, where the love of Christ will be experienced, and where Christ's purpose for our lives will be discovered.

MINISTER: In the name of our Saviour Christ I install you as officers and teachers in _____ United Church School. May you experience God's guidance and find joy in God's service.

R. B. Werry, 1986

A Commitment to Learning, at the Beginning of a New Church School Year

LEADER: We go on learning every day of our lives or we suffocate. In every human undertaking we have to learn again.

ADULTS: At every stage of living we must be open to newness and memory.

CHURCH SCHOOL TEACHERS AND YOUNG PEOPLE: Each of us has experience and insights to share. Often, however, we feel inadequate, and fear is our middle name.

LEADER: But our baptized name is Christian.

ALL: Therefore we share leadership and learning.

CHURCH SCHOOL TEACHERS AND YOUNG PEOPLE: We all have something to give and something to receive.

ALL: We pledge ourselves to each other, to this gathered community, to our necessary tasks. We commit ourselves to learn and learn again. We need you, God. We need each other. We are here for this.

LEADER: Amen.

Bloor Street United, Toronto, Ont., 1991

The Tree of Thanks

CHARACTERS: four children (CH) as the main actors; the rest of the church school.

MATERIALS: a good-sized bush or the branch of a tree, without leaves, large enough to hold a "leaf" for every person present at worship; a Christmas tree stand to hold the bush/branch; paper leaves made of autumn-coloured construction paper, one for each member of the congregation; pencils/pens for the congregation.

(CH 1 and 2 enter from the back of the sanctuary, carrying the tree.)

CH 1: Where are we going to put this tree?

CH 2: How about over by the pulpit?

CH 1: No, we can't put it there.

(CH 3 enters.)

CH 3: What are you two doing?

CH 1: _____ *(CH 2's name)* wants to put this tree by the pulpit!

CH 3: Well, why not? I think that's okay.

CH 1: What is this tree, anyway? It's too early for Christmas!

(CH 4 enters.)

CH 4: Will the three of you stop arguing and put that tree where it goes!

CH 1: Where?

CH 4: Don't you ever listen?

CH 1: I guess not. Where does it go?

CH 4: See that spot right there? *(Points to tree stand by the pulpit)* Put it there, in that stand.

CH 1: Okay. *(Puts tree in place, others help)* Now what do we do?

CH 2: _____ *(CH 4's name)*, don't you remember that _____ *(CH 1's name)* was absent last week when we were talking about this? That's the reason she doesn't know about this tree.

CH 4: I'm sorry. I forgot. *(Speaks to CH 1)* Well, it's not a Christmas tree; it's a Thanksgiving tree. Last week we wrote on a bunch of paper leaves all the things for which we are thankful.

CH 3: Now we're going to decorate our Thanksgiving tree. *(Turns to CH 2)* Okay, you can go and tell the others that we're ready.

(CH 2 goes off and returns with the entire church school. Each child has a leaf with things they are thankful for written on it. They come to the chancel and wait.)

CH 4: We're all ready now. _____ *(CH 3's name)*, you begin.

(All the children, with help of teachers if necessary, place leaves on tree.)

LEADER: Our Thanksgiving Tree is beginning to blossom! Everyone has something to be thankful for. Today we are going to offer our prayers of thanksgiving a little differently than we do on other Sundays. As each of you came in, you were given a small leaf. Take a moment, now, prayerfully, to consider those things you are thankful for. Write them down on your leaf. And when you are ready, come forward and place your leaf on our Thanksgiving Tree.

(When all have placed their leaves on the tree, the regular offering is gathered and the following offertory song, to the tune "Come, ye thankful people come," is sung.)

We have brought our thanks today;
placed our blessings on display.
Now our blessings you can see
have been placed upon this tree.
We could name a whole lot more—
God sends blessings by the score.
God our Maker does provide;
all our needs are satisfied.

Helen Kitchell Evans, 1988

The Pumpkin as Sign of Thanksgiving

A large pumpkin is the central focus of the usual Thanksgiving display at the front of the sanctuary. At the Children's Time, it is lifted out of the display and placed on a small table or stool close to the congregation. Have ready a sharp knife and a towel (for wiping your hands later).

Message: Pumpkins make wonderful Thanksgiving Day symbols because pumpkins are useful both inside and out.

How is the outside of a pumpkin useful? It's decorative, good for Thanksgiving displays, can be made into pumpkin pies; when Halloween comes, it can be made into jack-o-lanterns.

Okay *(cut off top of pumpkin),* but pumpkins are not only useful on the outside *(pull out a handful of seeds and pulp and hold up for all to see),* pumpkins are useful on the inside as well. Pumpkins are full of seeds and these seeds, when planted, will become new pumpkins. So the seeds remind us of the promise of the renewal of life. Winter is coming; but winter will not last forever. Though things are dying or going south for the winter, hidden in the pumpkin, and hidden in almost everything in God's creation, is the promise of new life that will come in the spring.

So, pumpkins are a true symbol of thanksgiving, both inside and out. *(Conclude with prayer.)*

S/A, 1988

An Affirmation of Thankfulness

As a concluding act of thanksgiving I invite all to share in the Affirmation of Thankfulness printed in the order of service. First, take a moment to read over the words of the prayer. As you read, please identify the paragraph or phrase that best expresses your sense of thankfulness... *(pause for silent reading)*

Now, I invite you to join with me in making this Affirmation of Thanksgiving. We begin with all seated, but when we come to the paragraph or phrase that you have chosen, please stand as a means of expressing your personal thanksgiving. Hopefully the final phrase, "for all else that we name in our hearts," will get us all on our feet!

1. This day we affirm the faith of thankful spirits:
2. We are grateful to God, and would be found more grateful still.

1. For life and its mystery:
2. Our earth journeying through space and *our* journeying from birth to death and beyond.

1. For the turning seasons of the year, and for this season of harvest:
2. Crisp sunshine and trees aflame, tangy fruit on tree and vine, tables laden with turkey and golden gravy, sweet vegetables and pies, shining faces ready to feast.

1. For the fullness of gathered family:
2. Delight of children and banter of teens, rock music and worn jeans, steadying parents and loving partners, staying power through laughter and tears.

1. For the inheritance of faith:
2. The Word of God and the story of Jesus, the holy passion of prophets and pastors, the spirit of reverence and wonder and trust, the hope that cannot be extinguished, the love that will not let us go.

1. For the holiness of beauty:
2. In music and colour, in dance and design.

1. For quiet and solitude:
2. The privilege of the shut door, the companionship of a good book, walking in the light of the moon.

1. For useful work and the privilege of play:
2. And for all else that we name in our hearts.

1. Let God's people say:
2. Thank you! Amen!

Peter Wyatt, 1988

"Giving Makes Us Free": A Dramatic Discussion about Stewardship

MINISTER: *(begins sermon as usual, perhaps a bit more animated...)* "So God took the first person and placed him in the garden to till it and keep it." And it's been all downhill ever since. From a position of responsibility and trust, we humans have managed to totally destroy, rape, ruin, and pillage this garden we call Earth. All of us sit here this morning as thieves who have robbed this world and its people so that we can drive the cars that sit in the parking lot, wear the expensive clothes on our backs, and return to the wasteful inefficient boxes we call houses. Furthermore, when we have a chance to reduce the wrongs of this world by giving freely to our Christian community, we fail to give enough time, money, or skills to enable the church to be an agent of redemption and healing in our broken world!

REGULAR GIVER: Nonsense! *(gets up and starts to leave...)*

MINISTER: What's wrong, _____ ? *(person's name)* Come back. Listen, I...

REGULAR GIVER: No, *you* listen. I resent what you are saying. I won't sit here and let you make us feel bad. This is *our* world and we have a right to live in it! God gave us the ability to create and use the world's resources responsibly and there's nothing wrong with that! You would have us return to the Garden of Eden—we were expelled, remember? I give of my time and resources to this congregation for the very reason you are suggesting, and it's not fair that you can get up there and

rant and rave at us like that. The issue is far more complex than what you are suggesting!

PEACE BUFF: *(positioned fairly close to the front so that s/he can direct her/his comments to REGULAR GIVER but also to the congregation; MINISTER looks shocked and surprised that things are getting out of hand)*: Hurrah! At last we have a minister who is brave enough to tell it like it really is! Have *you* *(addressing REGULAR GIVER)* ever tried to get someone to volunteer around here? Have *you* ever tried to get people committed or involved in the life of this church? It's impossible! It's always the same old faces doing the same old jobs while 80 percent of our congregation sit back and complain.

NEWCOMER: *(seated towards the back, jumps up)* Hey, hold it! I'm a newcomer, and I didn't come here this morning to listen to all this bickering! Sounds to me like you're airing all your dirty linen! I came here this morning to worship. To have some quiet time. To leave the outside world out there *(gestures)* and have time with God. I didn't come to listen to this. What's this got to do with worship, anyway?

MODERATE: *(jumps up, points to NEWCOMER)* You're right! This should be a time to be inspired by God and to feel some healing in our lives. This should be a place where we can look around and feel comfortable and at home with people who care about us. We need to know that God is working in our lives. Yet, to be here just for ourselves seems a bit selfish and inward. The Bible tells us Jesus spent his time out on the street, being with people, healing them, when he wasn't worshipping God. Don't we have a responsibility too? I think we're *all* right in our own way, but we need to be open and listen to each other!

(MINISTER continues to look shocked and embarrassed, shakes her/his head....)

PEACE BUFF: *(directs first sentence to MODER-ATE, then turns and directs rest of comments to MINISTER)* Well, that's all very well and good, but where are you when we need volunteers? I work very hard trying to make a difference in the world and sometimes I feel very much alone. I desperately want to see everyone on this planet enjoy peace, health, and prosperity. I think if Jesus were living today he would be working hard to make that happen!

(MINISTER starts to reply but REGULAR GIVER takes over....)

REGULAR GIVER: But Jesus *isn't* here, and even if he were here this a different world than the one he lived in. We have to deal with technology and multinational corporations and world disasters that Jesus could not have envisioned. A simple "love your neighbour" simply isn't enough anymore!

(When REGULAR GIVER says "But Jesus isn't *here," PEACE BUFF interjects, "What do you mean, Jesus isn't here?", but REGULAR GIVER continues anyway.)*

MINISTER: That's precisely why the church should be supported and well funded. That's why we need your skills and insights, not just your money! That's why we need all of you! I think I better throw this sermon away *(throws sermon notes over shoulder)*. You're right! When I talk about these things up here, you just end up feeling guilty, or helpless, or mad. It's only when *all* of us struggle with being good stewards that real change can come about!

NEWCOMER: *(pointing to MINISTER and then to self)* Are you trying to tell me that I have to do more than just come to church on Sunday? Forget it! I won't bother you if you don't bother me. Besides, I have nothing to give. And even if I did, who would I talk to? By the way, what's a steward anyway?

MODERATE: I think I can answer that. Stewardship is a biblical word which means that we are responsible for this world *but*—we don't own it. It means that we have to take care of it for God and use its resources wisely. And somehow when we give of ourselves and share with one another, whether it's in our homes, offices, or out in the community, that's when we are fully alive and are the people God means us to be. When we realize that what we have is only on loan, it becomes much more precious to us. It's like our children. We know we can never own them, but we can cherish them and love them and help them to be the best they can be.

REGULAR GIVER: *(turns and comments to MODERATE)* You mean for me to be a good Christian, or "steward" as you call it, I need to live *all* my life, including my work, in an attempt to make this world a better place for everyone?

(Before MODERATE can answer, PEACE BUFF jumps in....)

PEACE BUFF: That's right! We need to see that what we do here on Sunday morning and throughout the week affects people in South Africa, Nicaragua, and right here in _____. We don't live in this world each to ourselves.

MINISTER: *(becoming visibly relieved)* Boy, am I glad to hear you talking about these things! I get so frustrated trying to get you to think about these issues without your getting upset at me. Just knowing we can talk about this gives me hope, and without hope we would all give up. This is what God's new community that Jesus spoke of is all about!

MODERATE: *(agreeing with MINISTER)* That's right! We need a vision of God's new community, and then we need to keep it before us. Every Sunday when we worship we are holding that vision up and asking God to make that new community real. Perhaps that's what we should be doing right now.

NEWCOMER: *(still looking a bit confused, but also relieved, says in thoughtful way)* Well, it's about time! I can't take any more of this! But, you've made me think. I'm not sure about a church that talks about God in one breath and social issues in the next, but maybe there's something to it. Please Reverend, how about a prayer?

MINISTER: All right. I guess that's a good idea. But I hope people will realize that stewardship is about more than just money and will look at our displays and come to our congregational dinners in October.
Now, let's join in prayer... *(all but Minister are seated)*.

Gay Petkau, 1985

"Faith and Action": A Stewardship Dialogue

SCRIPTURE: James 2:14-26

RESPONSIVE READING:
This dialogue requires two readers, one with an unlit candle, the other with two unlit matches. Also required is an empty candlestick located centrally in the worship space.

1. I have this candle. It is sturdy and of good quality. It has the potential for many useful hours. However, this candle can serve only one purpose. It is not a key to unlock a door, nor is it a map to guide my travelling. Its only function is to give light, and for this it must be touched by fire. Without fire, the candle's potential purpose can never be realized.

2. I have this match. *(light one match)* It burns brightly and its flame is hot. The match changes whatever it touches, causing paper to burn or giving light in a dark place. However, this single match will quickly use up all its available fuel, and then it must go out. *(let the match burn out)* It cannot burn forever all alone because it does not have of itself the necessary resources for a long life. Only when the match touches a lamp, or a candle, can its flame go on burning at length and become a useful, reliable tool.

1. So I offer you this candle. *(hold candle out to Reader 2)*

2. And I offer you this match. *(light second match)*

1. *(while Reader 2 lights candle)* And in joining together both the candle—like our lives—

2. ... and the match—like our faith—we can fulfil their purposes and achieve long-lasting effects.

(Leave lighted candle in candleholder, burning throughout the rest of the service.)

GROUP A: We are Faith. We trust God completely. We can move mountains. We can make people whole. Though we begin as small as a tiny mustard seed, we can grow into a large, significant force.

GROUP B: We are Action. We want to get things done. We can travel great distances. We can touch all types of people. We can use many hands and together accomplish mighty tasks.

A: We are Faith. We wait for miraculous answers to our numerous prayers. But from the grandeur of our churches and the safety of our homes, we wonder why God does not respond. This causes us to doubt.

B: We are Action. We organize great ventures, covering all logistical problems, but—our motivation drops, our enthusiasm dies, and we become exhausted.

A: God wants our faith to be displayed in what we do. Faith without action is lifeless.

B: God wants our actions to reflect *God's* desires—not *our* plans. Action without faith loses its meaning.

A: God wants our faith to live through our actions.

B: God wants our actions to be inspired by our faith.

ALL: Let us join faith and action together in God's work in our world.

UNISON PRAYER:

O God, you know that we sometimes sing our hymns but do not live out their words. You know how often we pray for help but ignore your commands if they do not suit us well. Forgive us. Help our lives to reflect what we learn of you in scripture. Help our actions to be in accord with your loving purposes. Help us in our struggle to be Christ-like in both word and deed. Give us opportunities in the days ahead to put our faith into action in helpfulness to all around us.

Wendy Howie, 1989

About All Saints' Day

The commemoration of the days on which martyrs died was an important part of early church worship. By the fifth century, however, there were too many martyrs to fit into the calendar, and there was a concern that some of the martyrs had been forgotten. So a general All Martyrs' (eventually All Saints') Day was instituted. Originally this celebration was associated with the Easter season, but was moved to November 1 in the ninth-century reform of the calendar.

Martyr means "witness" in Greek. Martyrs are those who have borne witness to the faith. "Saints," on the other hand, is a term used in the Pauline writings to describe all the people of God ("the saints at Corinth," etc.) We need to get away from the popular notion of "plaster saints," those whose lives are so pure they are almost inhuman. (I remember a George Bernard Shaw line: "She was so heavenly-minded she was no earthly good!") All Saints' is a time to remember the great ones of the church, not because they were more holy than us, but because they have led the way in witnessing to the faith.

Choose six or seven saints of the church: St. Mary Magdalene (the first "witness" to the resurrection), St. Francis of Assisi, or St. Clare of the Poor Clares, St. Theresa of Avila (see the *Penguin Dictionary of Saints*); a Reformation "saint" such as Martin Luther, Katherina Schuetz-Zell, or John Knox (send $5 to the Vancouver School of Theology and ask for Gerald Hobbs' book, *Portraits of Spirituality*); a Canadian saint such as John McDougall, Chief Poundmaker, Nellie McClung (check out the old "New Curriculum" books); a modern saint, such as Martin Luther King, Jr., Oscar Romero, or Mother Teresa; and perhaps include a saint or two from your own congregation.

Send families to the library to search out information. Have a member of each family read a thumbnail sketch of their saint as part of a litany (edit these to keep them short), each sketch ending with: "And so we pray that we might follow in the footsteps of _____ who (outline one noteworthy characteristic of the person)." The people respond with: "God, hear our prayer."

A photographer in the congregation might make slides from pictures of the various saints. These could be shown on a screen during the litany. Or families might have made banners or posters representing each saint. A candle could be lit for each saint from the Christ candle and placed in an All Saints' candelabrum. The litany could end with an All Saints' (because we are all saints) procession around the sanctuary, to the tune "When the Saints go marching in."

Thomas Harding, 1990

Dedication of an Elevator for the Disabled

SCRIPTURE: Mark 2:2-5, 11-12

1. In the spirit of the friends who sought to break through to Jesus' life-giving presence,
2. We act today to enhance a ministry of access to the resources of this church.

1. We recognize and celebrate the vision and commitment of those who have supported this project to completion.
2. We rejoice in the work of these friends and offer them our gratitude.

1. We confess the ways we continue to exclude others from the community of faith, through our structures, prejudices, or ignorance.
2. We dedicate ourselves again to the world-loving Spirit of Christ, to the justice and peace of God's love.

1. In gratitude for the gifts of the Spirit and in hope for the life of Christ's ministry, we dedicate this new elevator for the disabled to the glory and service of God.
2. Amen.

1. Let us pray—
2. We praise you, O God, for the gifts of your love, which open our eyes to new horizons. You offer a place for each person in your grace. Bless us in this act and help us to serve you in our common life, through Jesus Christ our Saviour.

Rob Johns, 1986

Dedication of Communion Ware

SCRIPTURE: Psalm 100

(The candlesticks are brought to the Table.)

1. Let us recall the words of our Saviour:
2. "I am the light of the world. Whoever believes in me will have the light of life."
1. Bless, O God, these candlesticks, that those who worship here may be illuminated by your truth.

(The patens are brought to the Table.)

1. Let us recall the words of our Redeemer:
2. "I am the bread of life. Whoever believes in me will never hunger."
1. Bless, O God, these patens, that those who worship here may be nourished by your grace.

(The chalices are brought to the Table.)

1. Let us recall the words of our great high priest:
2. "I am the true vine. Whoever abides in me will bear much fruit."
1. Bless, O God, these chalices, that those who worship here may be revived by your power.

(The flask is brought to the Table.)

1. Let us recall the words of our Shepherd:
2. "I am the living water. Whoever believes in me will become an unending spring."
1. Bless, O God, these vessels, that those who worship here may be witnesses to your love.

Sylvia Dunstan, 1989

HYMNS FOR THE AUTUMN

An Anniversary Sunday Hymn

(Hymn to Joy, 8 7 8 7 D)

God we thank you, God we praise you
that you've brought us to this hour,
and that we have journeyed safely
guided by your Spirit's power.
At this time of anniversary
may we now to you draw near,
off'ring prayers and songs of gladness
for another grace-filled year.

God of time and God of history
you are first and you are last:
Keep alive the sacred story
of the saints in ages past—
those who built this congregation
with the labours of their hands,
and the faithful generations
of your church in many lands.

God of earth's unfolding present,
now descend to us we pray:
Move us to accept the challenge
that confronts your church today.
Earth is broken, hearts are breaking,
your world thirsts to be renewed.
Channel your divine compassion
through the lives we give to you.

God of hope, the earth's tomorrow,
may we your disciples be:
Filled with hope that never falters,
help us live courageously.
As we pause along the journey
on the pathway you have laid,
Strong Protector, may we ever
face the future unafraid.

Paul Miller/Diane Walker, 1985

O God, you are a dwelling-place

(Warrington, 8 8 8 8)

O God, you are a dwelling-place
where troubled souls their wandering cease.
Your arms provide a sheltering space
and you surround us with your peace.

When simple Christians broke your earth
to fashion this, our house of prayer,
they built a cradle of rebirth,
a haven of your tender care.

Across the years this church has stood,
a sign of faith, a place of love.
And still we celebrate the good
that joins our hearts with yours above.

We are your dwelling-place, O God;
you build us up, restore us whole.
The seeds of faith you cast abroad
take root in soil of eager souls.

So as we look to future years
may you our joy and hope renew.
Your perfect love casts out our fears:
You live in us and we in you.

Paul Miller/Diane Walker, 1985

For the bounty of the oceans
(All the Way, 8 7 8 7 D)

For the bounty of the oceans,
for the fruitfulness of earth,
for the love of friends and family
from the moment of our birth,
for the skills of arts and science
lifting spirit, easing strain,
for the wonders that surround us,
praise, O God, be to your name.

For destruction of your rivers,
for the ravishing of earth,
for the careless quest for profit,
heedless of creation's worth,
for abuse of craft and insight,
crushing promise, seeking gain,
for the desolation round us,
we ask pardon in your name.

For the heritage of freedom,
for the precious sense of place,
for the sacrifice of others,
selfless channels of your grace,
for the carers and the sharers,
giving comfort, treating pain,
for the Christ who suffering for us,
we give thanks in his dear name.

In the clamour of the nations,
in the clash of class and race,
all the little ones who suffer
shattered by the modern pace,
all the hungry and the homeless,
cast aside, left in disdain,
all these victims of injustice
we commend unto your name.

May we bear each other's burdens,
may we go forth in your grace,
may the harmony of heaven
come to birth in time and space,
may your kingdom and your power,
shown in Christ who lives again,
may your care for all creation
render glory to your name.

Colin Grant, 1989

Source of light and cosmic force
(England's Lane, Dix, 7 7 7 7 7 7)

Source of light and cosmic force,
God of earth and sea and sky:
you have set our human course,
ever seeking how and why.
But your gift of will that's free
begs responsibility.

Source of life, whose likeness lives
in the mingling cell and gene;
God of time, your nurt'ring gives
growth to life that's yet unseen.
We would be both true and just
in this procreative trust.

Source of love, whose child became
Lord of life through human birth—
sanctity of life reclaimed,
giving every soul its worth.
Holy love, that touches all,
make us faithful to your call.

© 1983, 1992 *Doreen Lankshear-Smith*

God speaks to us

(Kingsfold, 8 6 8 6 D)

God speaks to us in varied ways
while on life's path we tread;
from sun-lit peak and crested wave
each hungry soul is fed.
In dappled skies, in coloured leaf,
the seasons cast their spell
like magic carpets on the earth;
with God all things are well.

God speaks to us in varied ways,
through parent, teacher, friend,
who through the daily pilgrimage
their gifts of love extend:
the constant care, the steadfast hope,
the witness that they show
in sacrificial ways, that we
a fuller life may know.

In varied ways God speaks to us
that we may hear the voice
of one who comes to be the Way,
the Truth, the Light, the Life.
The name is Jesus—Saviour, Friend,
whose daily grace we seek
to give us strength and health and joy,
that we to God may speak.

S. R. Purchase, 1991

Stewardship Hymn

(St. Peter, 8 6 8 6)

O God, in Christ your best you gave,
your love and grace to share,
and called from us an answ'ring love
to bless all, everywhere.

You call your church, in every place,
through all we do and are
to carry on the work of grace
for people near and far.

To give according to our means
shares grace with all around;
to freely give beyond our means
helps miracles abound.

O God, we give our lives to you,
responsive to your call;
for when we give ourselves to you,
we give the best of all.

Glen Baker, 1989

A Stewardship Hymn

(Stuttgart, 8 7 8 7)

God of ageless, matchless beauty,
God of darkness and of sun:
send your stewards to their duty
to enfold the earth as one.

Yours the voice of prophet's wisdom,
yours the realm of dreams untold;
countless people glimpse your kingdom
when we seek to share, not hold.

In this age of evil's raging,
in our conflict's bitter strife:
grant your peace through our engaging
so that nations find new life.

With our labour and our leisure,
with our time and talent's fruit:
cause us to embrace full measure
purposes that grow and root.

You who grant us gifts unnumbered,
author of the earth's design:
wake us, shake us from our slumber,
make of us your living sign.

Brian MacIntosh, 1987

It was in the beginning

(Lancashire, 7 6 7 6 D)

It was in the beginning
that God made something new,
and those on earth were given
a task for each to do.
The soil was ploughed and planted,
the sea brought forth her fruit;
God saw the union working
and then pronounced it good.

Too soon there was dissension
as greed and hunger grew,
and God warned all the people
what they would have to do.
But most ignored God's wisdom,
and soon the flood began;
God's tears were like the raindrops
that covered up the land.

The rain came down in torrents
for forty nights and days,
then God set in the heavens
a sign which Noah praised:
A rainbow showed God's mercy,
a promise of goodwill,
and life moved ever onward,
with God creating still.

So as in the beginning
God gave us something new—
a world to love and honour,
a sacred trust and true.
And still we seek to follow
the path where God will lead,
as God and all creation
seek unity indeed.

Judith Vaclavik, 1991

All these lived by faith

(Austria, 8 7 8 7 D)

For the faithful who have answered
when they heard your call to serve,
for the many ways you led them
testing will and stretching nerve,
for their work and for their witness
as they strove against the odds,
for their courage and obedience
we give thanks and praise, O God.

Many eyes have glimpsed the promise,
many hearts have yearned to see,
many ears have heard you calling
us to greater liberty.
Some have fallen in the struggle;
others still are fighting on.
You are not ashamed to own us.
We give thanks and praise, O God.

For this cloud of faithful witness,
for the common life we share,
for a world of peace and justice,
for the gospel that we bear,
for the vision that our homeland
is your love: deep, high and broad,
for the different roads we travel,
we give thanks and praise, O God.

Sylvia Dunstan, 1985

Dedication of Offering

(Edelweiss)

God of love, hear our prayer:
bless this offering we bring you.
May our lives do your will;
guide and guard us forever.
Give us courage to stand for truth;
help us care for others.
God of love, hear our prayer:
bless this offering we bring you.

S/A, 1988

O God of peace

(Ellers, 10 10 10 10)

O God of peace dwell in our midst today.
Still now the anguish of our fearful way.
Unclench the fists of anger, hurt and pride.
Banish the noise of war on ev'ry side.

O Source of breath, whose loving power unites
all of earth's creatures in a common life:
Give us the grace to touch the world with care
and share with all the gifts created there.

Grant us no rest from purpose in your grace;
to seek for peace and justice in the place
where you have set our feet and steeled our nerve,
with laughter, gentleness and love to serve.

Give courage now, O Christ, when dark appears;
help us stand fast in honest doubt and fears.
Give to your children as they work and wait
life of the Spirit filled with costly grace.

Rob Johns, 1986

The prophets had a vision

(Aurelia, 7 6 7 6 D)

The prophets had a vision
of what could come to be,
of righteousness and justice,
and of integrity.
They saw for God's whole people
a time for fear to cease,
with swords beat into ploughshares
and neighbours learning peace.

It is a call to travel
away from guarded walls;
to follow God's own pathway,
to listen where God calls.
To lean not on our armies
nor trust in our own might:
O house of Jacob! Pilgrims!
Trust in the Lord's great light.

This vision still reminds us,
though years have come between,
that we, like they, are pilgrims,
despite what we have seen.
Reality surrounds us,
for safety's sake we stay,
while dreams of change confound us
and beckon us away.

God's kingdom grows within us
and wrong gives way to right;
and we who once were darkness
have now become the light.
Our pilgrimage unending
bears fruit as we go on.
The message we are sending
is this: "God's will be done!"

Doug Norris, 1990

May we have the eyes of Jesus

(St. Oswald, 8 7 8 7)

May we have the eyes of Jesus,
see injustice where we live;
freeing captives from their prisons,
courage and compassion give.

May we have the mind of Jesus,
see life from Christ's point of view:
each a child of God accepted,
all creation to renew.

May we have the hands of Jesus,
outstretched in untiring care;
raising up the sad and lonely,
helping heavy burdens bear.

May we have the heart of Jesus,
filled with everlasting love;
ever-giving and forgiving,
to reflect our God above.

Margaret Beatty, 1985

PRAYERS FOR THE AUTUMN

Prayers of the Day (Collects)

O God, whose glory is sung by heavenly choirs and by earthly refugees, in soaring anthems and in falling leaves: Give us grace this day to hear your still small voice, that we may be moved to deeper reverence, broadened love, and blossoming hope; through Jesus Christ, to whom with you and the Spirit, one holy God, be honour and praise, now and forever.

Peter Wyatt, 1989

Eternal God, not of the dead, but of the living: We give you thanks and praise for all the faithful people who, having served you here in holiness and love, are now with you in glory. Enable us so to follow them in faithful service that we may, with them, behold you face to face in your eternal kingdom, one with them forever; through Christ our Saviour.

Emmanuel United, North Bay, Ont., 1991

God of the nations: You have called us into your community from the ends of the earth. Strengthen our faith and give us the peace which passes understanding; through Jesus Christ the Prince of Peace, to whom with you and the Spirit, one holy God, be honour and praise, now and forever.

Maggie Muldoon-Burr, 1991

God of holy terror, from whom we flee, whose silence burns like ice, whose Word we long to hear: Speak to our isolation, that we may recognize your voice beyond our emptiness. Enfolded by your Word, empowered by your presence, may we go forth in justice and in joy to embrace your aching world; through Jesus Christ, to whom with you and the Spirit, one holy God, be honour and praise, now and forever.

Paul Fayter, 1991

Calls to Worship

1. We are called to be the church, to love God and serve others.
2. We gather as sisters and brothers in Christ, praising God's faithfulness, embracing each other in God's love, committed to acting out that love in God's world.
1. We worship God in joy, in expectation, and in hope.
2. We are not alone. Thanks be to God!

William Phipps, 1982

1. In the beginning was the Word:
2. And creation unfolded at God's direction.
1. In the beginning was the Word:
2. And the prophets spoke by God's direction.
1. In the beginning was the Word:
2. And Christ lived that Word to God's glory.
1. May God's Word be spoken, heard, and celebrated today.

Douglas Flint, 1984

1. May the God of Israel, who led God's people to a promised land, also lead us.
2. And bring us to a place of blessing.
1. Let us worship God.

Gordon Churchill, 1985

1. We give thanks to God for all God's goodness.
2. God's steadfast love endures forever.
1. Once we were a wandering people, hungry and thirsty in a desert land. But we cried to God for deliverance, and were led to a new land rich in promise and harvest.
2. God satisfies the thirsty, feeds the hungry, leads us through the desert to a harvest home.
1. Come, let us worship God.

Whitman Strong, 1987

1. Come, ye joyful people, come!
2. God has created the earth and all that is in it.
1. God's glory echoes through all creation. Scarlet maples, raucous crows, hardy fall flowers: all proclaim God's holy name.
2. God's love surrounds us. The laughter of children, the smile of a friend, the touch of a mother's hand: all affirm God's love.
1. Come, ye joyful people, come!
2. We come in thanksgiving to worship God our Creator.

Pat Milliken, 1991

Prayers of Approach

O God, we come a little bit from habit, a little bit from longing, a little bit for no particular reason at all. But now that we are here, it is good. We need the community, we need the celebration, we need the startlingness of your Word.

Keep us open, honest, and responsive in this hour. Then send us out again to be new creations in your desperate and wonder-filled world.

Beaverlodge United, Beaverlodge, Alta., 1978

Every part of creation is a hymn of praise to your greatness, O God. Every person is a statement of faith about your care and claiming love in Christ. Every thought, word, and action is evidence of the power of your Spirit. Claim again your creation, each one of us, and all our energies, for goodness' sake.

Don Waldon, 1984

Fit us, O God, for this new day. Through your Spirit, grant us courage so that its uncertainties may not overwhelm us. Through your Christ, fill us with love so that our differences may not divide us. Through your creative energy, make us new so that the past may not enslave us. Spirit, Christ, Creator, lead us into newness of life.

S/A, 1984

God of each new day: We come in worship seeking again to hear the good news of your unceasing love. May that love permeate every aspect of our living. Grant that our worship may renew us, and that our lives may participate in the renewal of your world. We ask this as your people, and because you are our God.

Laura J. Turnbull, 1988

Giver of light and life, we would be made whole again in your presence for we have been drained by this week. We would see again your glory and offer our praise for we have lost touch in the hurry of our days. We would renew our faith and commit again our lives as you have called us to do, in Jesus' name.

Terry Shillington, 1990

1. Our ears are full of the surge of combines, the chatter of children, the drone of the fridge, the blare of sirens, the jangle of the phone, constant television ... and we yearn for silence and a time when we do not have to respond to noise.
2. O God, hearer of every silent prayer, every cry of anguish, every song of joy: Train our ears to focus

on the words of life sung and spoken in worship this morning. Re-tune our lives that we may be receptive to your Word and hear again your call to life and service in Christ's name.

Dawn Ballantine-Dickson, 1990

God of all our days, always you are with us. You have laughed at the joy of new birth and mourned a needless death. In the laughing and the crying, the shouting and the silence, the anger and the hope, you have blessed us with your presence, moved us with your Spirit, upheld us with your love. Be with us now in this time of worship, we ask in Jesus' name.

Jack Ballantine-Dickson, 1991

Gracious God, we ask your blessing in and through this time of worship. May we be open to your presence and accept the gifts of your Spirit. Touch our lives in order that we may live to your honour and praise, this day and always.

Pat Milliken, 1991

Invitations to Confession

Sisters and brothers, as we prepare again to hear God's Word and receive again the mystery of God's love in bread and wine, let us acknowledge our sin and ask God's pardon and strength.

If we say we have no sin we deceive ourselves and the truth is not in us. But if we confess our sin, God is faithful and just and will forgive our sin and cleanse us from all unrighteousness. Let us make our confession, now, in the presence of a gracious God.

When we gather in the presence of God we have the opportunity to see ourselves as God sees us. We can see how our faults and failure have broken right relationship with others, with God, and with our best selves. Let us offer to God those areas of our lives

that are in need of healing and forgiveness. Let us come in confession.

We are the household of God, a chosen people, a royal priesthood, and yet: the good that we would we do not, and the evil we would not we do. Let us make our confession now before the God of forgiving love.

S/A, 1985

Prayers of Confession

God of harvests and of new beginnings: We confess those things which keep us from the life you offer. We bring what is hurtful and unfinished about summer—partings and failures, angry moments and tasks undone. We confess these bruises on our spirits... *(silent prayer)*

And we bring our resistances, O God: the pride that keeps us from asking forgiveness, the lack of energy that turns us away from new adventures, spirits too clogged to wonder and to pray. We confess our unwillingness to risk for the future... *(silent prayer)*

Unburden us, lighten us, free us, we pray. Grant us forgiveness, in Jesus' name.

Terry Shillington, 1990

Forgive us, God, for failing to put our minds and spirits in harness to cut the furrow in which you might plant your seed. We look to you for answers to world hunger, war, injustice, yet refuse to yoke ourselves to the discipline of Christ which speaks of acting justly, sharing our abundance, praying fervently, living expectantly.

O God of the greatest harvest, who sows the Spirit within us, let our actions be rooted in our faith, and produce the fragile fruit of love which brings your new community into being, one prayer, one shared sorrow, one simple act of justice at a time.

Dawn Ballantine-Dickson, 1984

Healing God, we see the sin and pain of the world reflected in our own lives: the suffering that longs for comfort, the brokenness that yearns for wholeness, the hunger that craves nourishment. Yet we, like the world, so often choose to ignore the sin and pain: to close our eyes, to turn our backs, to run away.

In your mercy, call us back to your ways. Give us strength to confess, courage to repent, and grace to change.

Ed Lewis, 1985

O God who knows our innermost nooks and crannies, you have seen how busy we are in looking successful and attractive, calm and in control. Yet you know, also, the turmoil inside us. To you we name the places where we hurt, where we have failed, where we are ashamed. To you we name the fears we have about tomorrow: for ourselves, for those we love, for our world. To you we name our doubts and our uneasiness in responding to your call... *(silent prayer)*

Come to us with healing power, O God. Fill us with your life-giving Spirit, we pray.

Terry Shillington, 1990

God, we are tired of feeling helpless when we think of your world, its hurt and its brokenness. We are tired of starving children and weeping mothers, of parched soil and polluted streams. We are tired of polls and politicians, of angry poverty and comfortable wealth, of sixty-cent coffee and three-dollar wheat.

Forgive our exhaustion, O God. Renew our compassion. Give us the courage to keep going, with hearts and hands wide open in love.

Jack Ballantine-Dickson, 1990

Creator, Redeemer, Sustainer God: So often we search for comfort and resist your challenge. We fill ourselves with the goodness of our gardens and hunger for the bread that would satisfy our spirits. We have been so concerned with making a living that we have missed the abundant life you offer. Forgive our unfaithfulness. Teach us to turn again to you who provides us with every good thing according to your loving purposes.

Have mercy, O God. Grant the strength and courage to begin again.

Dawn Ballantine-Dickson, 1990

Most gracious and caring God, we turn to you trusting in your unfailing compassion. We acknowledge before you that our thoughts, actions, and words have betrayed the trust and commitment to which we are called. Free us from our guilt and guide us in your way of faithfulness; we pray in Jesus' name.

Laura J. Turnbull, 1991

Tickles of discomfort disrupt our evening solitude. Creeping unease visits us between closing our eyes and drifting off to sleep. You know the way of our hearts, our lips, our fickle selves. We have not been friends with all alike. We have given in to anger, impatience, even (we are ashamed to pray it) to despising all too easily. Visit us now in the bright light of morning with some way, some one to whom to make amends... *(silent prayer)*

Break now our guilt like a troublesome twig, O God. Brush aside our remorse like yesteryear's cobwebs. May we be friends with the world again, gladsome in fresh grace to love boldly and sin no more.

Robin Wardlaw, 1991

Assurances of Pardon/Forgiveness

As we have opened ourselves to God, so God has accepted us. Indeed, even before we are alive to the divine possibility, God has accepted us. In the assurance that we matter to God, that we are accepted as we are, may we offer ourselves to lives of greater meaning and care.

Bill Steadman, 1984

1. God accepts, forgives, and empowers. We are set free from the domination of sin, set free to risk for God's kingdom of compassion, justice, and peace.
2. Thanks be to God for God's forgiveness, empowerment, and call.

Bill Phipps, 1985

When Christ sets us free for freedom, the future opens before us. Our lives are returned to us as gifts—gifts to be used for the coming of God's true community. Thanks be to God for both gift and challenge.

Paul Fayter, 1985

1. People of God, rejoice! In Christ there is forgiveness and freedom; in Christ there is empowerment and peace.
2. In Christ all things are made new. We are God's forgiven people. Thanks be to God!

Paul Fayter, 1988

Sisters and brothers: In spite of who we are, no matter what we have done, God leads us into freedom and wholeness. Accept God's forgiving love. Forgive one another. Come alive in Christ!

Bill Steadman, 1990

We are not now what we have been; nor are we yet what, by God's grace, we shall become. God hears our prayers, sets us free, strengthens us for service. Receive God's forgiveness. Thanks be to God!

Paul Fayter, 1991

Hear the good news of Jesus Christ: We are forgiven and we are loved. We need not succeed, nor achieve, nor win. We need only accept the fact that we are accepted. Thanks be to God!

Don Robertson, 1991

1. Be assured of God's continuing love. God forgives, accepts, and liberates us to be God's servant people in the world.
2. We do not have to justify ourselves, seek power, or worry about our self-worth; we are loved and accepted. Thanks be to God!

Bill Phipps, 1984

Offertory Prayers

Loving God, we offer our gifts to you. Here is the hope of our hearts, the excitement of our dreams, the way of our faith, the gift of our lives. We offer all that we are to you who are all that we have.

Don Robertson, 1991

Merciful God, in whom we live and move and have our being: Grant that these offerings may be acceptable as symbols of our lives and selves. May we be filled by your Spirit which enlivens all creation, discerning your precious presence everywhere. This we ask in the name of the One who is your gracious presence and most precious gift.

John Haynes, 1992

We bring our gifts confidently to you, O God, believing that your blessing will be clearly shown—in renewed lives, in joyful hearts, in hope restored, in community strengthened—as it was clearly shown in Jesus.

David Sparks, 1992

Loving Provider: You have met us in our need and supplied us with such abundant blessings. Enable us to continue to trust in your providence, that in our giving we may be faithful witnesses to your loving generosity. This we ask through Jesus Christ, your most gracious gift.

Linda Saffrey, 1992

Invitations to Prayer

God calls us to be a praying people. Let us join in prayer, offering our praise, thanksgivings, and intercessions to God.

God is the One who makes us, loves us, and sustains us. God is the One who makes, loves, and sustains the world. Let us offer ourselves and our world to God in prayer.

Faith is the assurance of things hoped for, the certainty of things unseen. We live by faith; we are saved by faith. In faith, let us bring our concerns to God in prayer.

Nothing can separate us from the love of God in Christ Jesus. In trust and confidence let us pray to the God of love.

Jesus said, "You will know the truth and the truth shall set you free." Let us seek God's truth and God's will for our lives and our world as we come in prayer.

S/A, 1985

Prayers of Thanksgiving and Intercession

Merciful, all-knowing God, full of days and rich in blessings: Accept our praise and thanksgiving in this season of surpassing beauty. Fruit of earth fills barn and bin, and fruit of the spirit surrounds us in inexhaustible abundance. You are truth and joy to us, our Friend and Lover.

Yet our world is not complete. The building of justice and peace in human hearts and human affairs is not finished. We grieve with victims of the hatred, greed, apathy, or sheer stupidity of others. We long for justice for minority communities, for racial groups, for women, for the disabled. In our homes, tension and anger linger unresolved, affection waxes and wanes, roles distribute work inequitably. Again we pray, O God, that justice be done, in the context of forgiveness, in *our* homes as in all homes.

Favour your people with strength sufficient for the day, so to stand up to the overbearing and to stoop to those in need. May we participate in the miracle of the ongoing incarnation of Christ, through the power of the Holy Spirit, in us, in our church, in our world, in this day.

Robin Wardlaw, 1987

Blessed God, hear us as we lift our thanks for the life and meaning, the dignity and hope you offer in Jesus Christ; for your steadfast, saving love and Holy Spirit; for our homes and families and friends; for care and peace and justice where they can be found; and for our mission to bring care and peace and justice where they cannot be found.

Hear us as we make intercession for your people throughout the world. For those who are beaten down, those who are without work, those who are in prison; for those who are old, or alone, or disabled, or stricken with grief. Strengthen, comfort, keep them by the healing presence of your Spirit.

Enable us to speak with Christ's voice, to work with Christ's hands in the midst of our world. May ours be lives through which Christ lives and works and reigns. Enable us to grow in spirit, faith, and love.

To you, God, be the glory, through Jesus Christ our Saviour, who taught us when we pray to say....

Paul Fayter, 1989

God our Maker and Redeemer: You have called us to gather in the name of Jesus and by the power of your Holy Spirit. You make us into one Body. We thank you for the church, for the written witness of your Word, for our life together in Christ. Give us hearts and minds and wills to love the unloved, the lonely, the afraid. Give us open arms and an activist faith for the sake of the hungry and the hurt, the oppressed and the poor. Help us to serve others without pride or self-interest, without a calculating spirit, that we might worship you in truth and integrity, and with joy, gladness, and gratitude.

God of grace, today especially we thank you for the men, women, and children who farm the land, and for workers everywhere who prepare and distribute food. Let us never forget the millions of people who are dying from hunger while we struggle to diet away our extra weight. Help us to find the wisdom and way to bring health and hope to our sisters and brothers. May we hasten the day when no one is hungry or ill because of our greed, or our neglect, or our worship of weaponry. May we hunger and thirst for righteousness alone; through Jesus Christ the Bread of Life and Wellspring of Living Water.

Paul Fayter, 1990

Prayers of the People

1. O God, we are here: wondering about you, wondering about our church, wondering about ourselves.

2. Is it possible, God, to really be the Church of Jesus Christ? We want so much to find meaning in our lives and world. We want to contribute as well as we are able to fullness for all our sisters and brothers. For our young people we desire purpose, challenge, and excitement in life. For those of us who are older we desire peace and security, the quiet confidence that our living and striving have been worthwhile. For our world we desire justice and equity, a new tomorrow.

1. Is it possible, God, to really be the Church of Jesus Christ?

2. Help us to explore together into the openness of your tomorrow. Give us courage to change where change is necessary. Give us wisdom to discover those things which can endure without changing. Break into our lives with your Word. Fill us with your Spirit. Blow freshness and fullness and newfound faith into our church in the weeks ahead.

1. Is it possible, God, to really be the Church of Jesus Christ?

2. That is your command, O God. Help us to obey it. That is your challenge, O God. Help us to accept it. That is our dream, O God. Help us to make it a reality.

1. Is it possible? Is it possible, O God?

Beaverlodge United, Beaverlodge, Alta., 1979

The following prayer focuses on what it means to be Christ's body in the world. Each paragraph of the prayer ends with the phrase, "The burden is great." The response to that phrase is, "We will share it!"

1. Creator God, you call us to be your Body in the world, your hands, your feet, your voice, your spirit. The burden is great:
2. We will share it!

1. So often we are tired. There are so many things that require our time and energy. Choices have to be made, priorities set. The burden is great:
2. We will share it!

1. We seek to be responsible for and supportive of one another. There is loneliness, pain, anguish, right here in _____. There seems to be so much sickness this fall and the economic insecurity which surrounds us frightens us all. The burden is great....

1. The world is troubled, full of violence and pain; there is hunger, injustice, oppression, war. We focus on peace, or on Central America, and yet there are so many other places and situations that need our prayers and concern. We feel so helpless in the face of the world's hurt. The burden is great....

1. We are your Body. Our gifts and talents, our time and energy, our very lives, when guided and knit together by you, are the means by which your purposes in the world are fulfilled. We need the wisdom, the insight, the courage to know where and how to offer our gifts and abilities. The burden is great....

1. God being our helper, we offer our lives and our church in a world of struggle and pain. We do this in Jesus' name, as Christ's body in the world.
2. Amen.

University Hill United, *Vancouver, B.C., 1985*

A Responsive Prayer of Covenanting Together

LEADER: Let us ask God for the grace to live in covenant with each other.... *(brief silence)*
Hear, O God, the prayers that come from our frailty. We seek to do your will in all things.

SIDE 1: Grant us the discipline to continue in prayer for one another.
SIDE 2: Grant us the courage to stand together in the face of opposition.

1: Grant us the wisdom to remain open to your voice in the voice of the church.
2: Grant us the insight to remain open to your voice in the voice of the world.

1: Grant us the humility that frees us from arrogance.
2: Grant us the strength to remain in community in the midst of conflict.

1: Grant us freedom from fear and worry that we may serve you with joy.
2: Grant us joy in each other that our fears and worries might be shared.

LEADER: All these gifts we need, O God, to remain in faithful covenant with each other and with you. Lead, help and comfort us with the presence of our Saviour, Jesus Christ.
ALL: Amen.

Sylvia Dunstan, *1988*

Prayers of Thanksgiving and Dedication

God of grace, creation and renewal: We are people who unwittingly take the many miracles of life for granted. We thank you for your wondrous gifts of clean air, clean water, wholesome food: those simple things upon which our lives depend. We thank you for your wondrous gifts of colour, sound, taste, aroma, texture, that delight our senses and add a special beauty to our days. We thank you for the gift of each other, and pray that we may truly treat each other as gifts from you.

Teach us to enjoy the wonder of life, O God. Receive these gifts we return to you in token of our thanksgiving. Use them and use us in love for your world.

Dawn Ballantine-Dickson, 1984

We give you thanks, gracious God, for all that we so often take for granted: for the air, the good earth and water which sustain life; for the joy of being part of a family and member of a circle of friends; for the privilege of joining others in a community of faith and the opportunity of prayer and praise; for the chance to learn and risk for justice and peace; and above all, for the knowledge that we are secure in your eternal love, made human in Jesus the Christ. Receive now the gifts we return to you....

Community Church, Terrace Bay, Ont., 1990

Commissionings and Benedictions

We are the servants of Christ, and Christ is in the world. Go forth, then, to serve those in whom Christ is present.

Bill Phipps, 1985

1. Go into the world, praising the God of creation.
2. We go forth in praise.
1. Go into the world, witnessing to the Risen Christ.
2. We go forth in witness.
1. Go into the world, empowered by the Holy Spirit.
2. We go forth in power.
1. Go into the world.
2. We go forth.

Sylvia Dunstan, 1985

Go in the knowledge that you are loved. Let love bear you up and carry you along. And may you be blessed: by God, the source of faithful love; by Christ, that Love Incarnate; and by the Spirit, who attests the truth of love to our hearts.

Peter Wyatt, 1988

Go forth, conscious of your calling as sent ones of the living Christ. Carry with you the authority of caring love.

Peter Wyatt, 1989

May the grace of God free you; may the Word of God empower you; may the love of God uphold you; may the needs of God's people inspire you; may the blessing of God enliven you as you go forth to be God's people in God's world.

David Sparks, 1990

1. Go now, remembering what we have said and done here. Go, remembering that we are a forgiven people, eternally loved, thoughtfully instructed, gratefully obedient, responding and being responsible wherever we are.
2. We go to be God's people in the world.
1. God's grace and peace go with you.

Don Daniel, 1990

Go into the world—too often profane and so often violent. Go in caring love, for it is still *God's* world. And may God Most High give you strength and courage and purpose as you go.

Peter Wyatt, 1988

As God brought us together, as God has been present in our worship, so God goes with us into the world. Go forth, open to God's leading in your lives.

Bill Steadman, 1992

1. Go into the world in faith.
2. We go, trusting God to lead us.
1. Go into the world in hope.
2. We go, with a vision of God's new age before us.
1. Go into the world in love.
2. We go, remembering that Christ died for all.
1. May the faithfulness of God, the love of Christ, and the hope which God's Spirit quickens within us, be with each one of us as we live out our faith this week.

Emmanuel United, Ottawa, Ont., 1976

PRAYERS FOR ANNIVERSARY SUNDAY

Calls to Worship

Another year has passed in the life of our congregation. Again we come to give thanks for this community of faith. May our coming together be in respect for those who have gone before us, in joy for those who are with us, and in concern for those who will come after us. As we have come together, let us pray....

Bill Steadman, 1984

1. O give thanks to God.
2. Whose love is eternal.
1. Who led Israel out of Egypt to freedom in the promised land.
2. God's love is eternal.
1. Who came in Christ, calling us into the church, promising to always be with us.
2. God's love is eternal.
1. Who sustained our parents in the faith, and will lead our children into the future.
2. God's love is eternal.
1. In times of trouble, in times of joy, in times of challenge, in times of comfort, God's love sustains us.
2. God's love is eternal.
1. Let us worship God.

Douglas Flint, 1986

Prayer of Approach

We come before you, God, on this Anniversary Sunday. Today we share memories of the church and our place in its life. We renew our commitment to the church as a gift from you. May your Spirit lead us into the future, as your presence has blessed us in the past. Be with us in our worship. Grant us with courage and vision, we pray.

Bill Steadman, 1989

Prayer of Confession

We confess, O God: that we have gloried in our achievements rather than glorifying you; we have enjoyed our private fellowship rather than opening our community to the lonely and needy; we have experienced our worship as duty rather than joy; we have considered our offerings a sacrifice, forgetting that all that we are and all that we have is yours. Come to us, God, with the healing power of forgiveness.

Judith Brocklehurst, 1985

Prayers of Thanksgiving and Intercession

God of all: for your Word contained in scripture, we give you thanks. For your good creation of which we are a part, we give you thanks. For the wild and spendthrift love you offer in Christ Jesus, we give you thanks. For this United Church of ours, and for our congregation; for people of faith wherever they are found, we give you thanks.

Forgive us all traces of self-righteousness. Pardon our misplaced anger. Forgive our tendency to exclude and patronize. Grant us wisdom to know when to speak with passion, when to listen with humility, when to be still and silently adore.

As we look at your world and our eyes are filled with scenes of desolation and despair, set our feet upon pathways of freedom and hope. Call us to conversion. Lead us—even if it be kicking and screaming—into the commonwealth of your new creation, where all are valued equally, where justice and peace embrace.

Grant us the holy courage to follow you, even into new and unfamiliar ways. Teach us to go forward by faith, and not by the wisdom of the world. For Jesus' sake, in whose name we ask it.

Paul Fayter, 1989

Commissioning and Benediction

May the God of those who have gone before us, the Christ whom they honoured, and the Spirit that propelled them, be with us, their children, this day and forever.

Harry Disher, 1992

PRAYERS FOR WORLDWIDE COMMUNION SUNDAY

Calls to Worship

1. This is God's world.
2. We come to worship our Creator and to celebrate the various gifts God has given us.
1. We share in the vision of a world joined as one family.
2. For the vision we are given and for the love that we share: Thanks be to God!

Bill Steadman, 1991

1. Come, let us praise the God who promises forgiveness of sin and fullness of grace.
2. Let us praise the Christ who is with us in times of trial and times of rejoicing.
1. Let us praise the Spirit who encourages us in the struggle for justice and peace.
2. Together with the church throughout all time and in all places, we praise the one God in worship.

Don Daniel, 1986

Prayers of Approach

The bread and the wine beckon to us, God. We gather with the taste of other communions vaguely on our lips, and ask for communion again.

Be new life to us. Fill us with love overflowing that we may be a means of grace to others. Visit our hungry hearts this day—in prayer, in praise, in Word, at Table. We ask this in the name of the One who was broken for us, poured out for us, in love.

Wes Ashwin, 1990

God, who nourishes us for the journey: It is strengthening to know that, as we gather at your table today, your people throughout the world are offering praise and thanksgiving as bread and wine are shared. May the mystery of your presence, experienced in our worship, bind us together into one worldwide community, through Christ our Host.

Camillia LaRouche, 1992

PRAYERS FOR THANKSGIVING SUNDAY

Prayer of the Day (Collect)

Creator of the fruitful earth: You have made us stewards of all your goodness. Give us hearts grateful for your many gifts and wills steadfast to use your bounty well, that the whole human family, today and in generations to come, may with us give thanks for the richness of your creation; through Jesus Christ, to whom with you and the Spirit, one holy God, be honour and praise, now and forever.

Paul Gibson, 1992

Calls to Worship

1. In our worship we are called to bring all that we are, all that we have, all that we hope for, all that we can be, in grateful thanksgiving.
2. We commit ourselves anew to God's purposes, grateful that God has given us life and filled our lives with fullness and with joy.
1. Come, let us worship; let us praise God's holy name.

Douglas Greenough, 1985

1. Praise be to God who created the earth and gives us the harvest.
2. God provides all that we need.
1. Praise be to God who surrounds us with love and strengthens us by the Holy Spirit.
2. God enriches our lives; God's care never ends.
1. People of God, we gather in worship.
2. Praise be to God!

Pat Milliken, 1992

Prayers of Approach

God our Creator, Redeemer, Sustainer: We come together before you today with grateful hearts and with songs of thanksgiving on our lips. May our worship be in spirit and in truth; may our hearts and minds be receptive to your Word; may our community we responsive to your call. We come as your thankful people; be with us as our gracious God.

Doug Martindale, 1987

O God, with early snowfall and late harvest, with financial pressures and threatened livelihood, with family heartaches and personal pain, we come to this time of thanksgiving. We know we have been richly blessed, but our problems stifle our gratitude.

Come to us as a refreshing breeze. Shine your radiant light on that which blocks our thankfulness. Strengthen us with your Spirit to face life's difficulties, and open us to the way of gratitude. We pray in the name of the One who is your greatest gift of all, the foundation of our thanksgiving.

Dawn Ballantine-Dickson, 1988

Prayer of Confession

God who creates us, Christ who redeems us, Spirit who renews us, hear our confession. As we gather on this Thanksgiving Day we know that others are in need. We live in a world in which a few take advantage of many, the rich take advantage of the poor, the full take advantage of the hungry. We give thanks for food and then eat too much. We give thanks for your love and then forget that we are your gifts of love to others.

Enable us to be the thankful people you would

have us be, O God. And open our lives to thankful action.

Don Daniel, 1990

Assurance of Pardon/Forgiveness

Sisters and brothers in Christ: God is abundant in love and plenteous in mercy. On this Day of Thanksgiving, delight in God's faithfulness—for we are a forgiven people. Thanks be to God!

Louise Mangan, 1991

Offertory Prayer

Creator God, whose loving hand has given us all that we possess: Grant us grace that we may honour you with our substance and, remembering the account which we must one day give, be faithful stewards of your bounty; through Jesus Christ, servant of all.

American Book of Common Prayer, adapted 1992

Prayers of the People

1. Creator of the land, the water, and the sky: Come and renew the face of the whole earth.
   O God, 2. Hear our prayer... *(silence)*

1. Giver of life, we are the sons and daughters of your holy breath. Give us new purpose to care in love for thc world of your making.
   O God, 2. Hear our prayer... *(silence)*

1. Saviour of the world: Touch our lips in the power of your new creation, that we may proclaim your gift of life.
   O God...

1. God of sparrows and wildflowers: Teach us to see and preserve the simple beauty of the gifts of your hand.
   O God...

1. Friend of the helpless and the poor: Strengthen the will of people everywhere to use your creation to the benefit of all.
   O God...

Paul Gibson, 1992

A Litany of Thanksgiving

1. For every breath we take, for every beat of our hearts, for every sensation of our bodies:
2. We give you thanks, O God.

1. For the ear that listens, for the hand that caresses, for the arms that reach out in love:
2. We give you thanks, O God.

1. For relief from pain, for the tears of shared sorrow, for the laughter of shared joy:
2. We give you thanks, O God.

1. For the freedom to choose, for the ability to love, for the power of hope:
2. We give you thanks, O God.

1. For the presence you reveal to us, for the courage you offer us, for the rest you assure us will be ours:
2. We give you thanks, O God.

Rob T. Smith, 1985

Commissioning and Benediction

Go forth, filled with thanksgiving:
thankful for the abundance God has given us,
thankful for God's gift of Godself in Jesus,
thankful for the purpose given to our lives
by God's call to be stewards of creation
and servants to the world.

Doug Martindale, 1987

PRAYERS FOR STEWARDSHIP SUNDAY

Call to Worship

1. The mission of the church began with Jesus who sent the disciples out to a world desperately in need of hope.
2. The mission of the church begins with people.
1. That mission continued through many generations as the good news was spread to the ends of the earth.
2. The mission of the church takes vision, courage and commitment.
1. That mission is ours today.
2. We gather in worship, open to God's call, seeking the courage, the resources, and the faith we need to be missioners in God's world.

Bill Steadman, 1986

Prayers of Approach

Loving God, with gracious purpose you have created us, placed us in your world, and called us to be care-takers of your earth. As we hear your Word this morning, enable us to renew our commitment to that call. Help us to wrestle with what it means to be faithful stewards of all that you have given us; through Christ our Saviour, who lives and reigns with you and the Holy Spirit, one God, now and forever.

St. Paul's United, Burnaby, B.C., 1983

Open our ears, O God, to hear what you are saying in the things that happen to us and to the people around us. Open our hands to do our work well and to help where help is needed. Open our lips to bring comfort, joy, and laughter, and to share your good news. Open our minds to discover new truths about you and our world. Open our hearts to love you and our neighbours as you have loved us.

Wendy Howie, 1989

A Litany (Revelation 21, 22)

1. Behold, I saw a new heaven and a new earth.
2. Give us that vision anew, O God. Open us to the prophets of our time who impatiently proclaim the newness that is yours.

1. Now God's home is with humanity. God will dwell with them and they shall be God's people.
2. Open us to the countless ways you dwell among us, God, loving us and our world into life.

1. Death will be no more, neither grief, nor crying, nor pain; for the former things have passed away.
2. Speak to us again of wild, impossible dreams, O God. Make us believers, radical dreamers for your coming community.

1. And the angel showed me the river of the water of life, flowing down the middle of the city's street.
2. How weary we are of doing good, O God. Cause us to drink of the living water flowing at our very feet; cause us to drink of the water that will never fail.

1. And on each side was the tree of life, its leaves for the healing of the nations.
2. Let us be leaves for the healing of the nations, God. Let us share in your reconciling, wholeness-making, newness-bringing work.

Terry Shillington, 1986

PRAYERS FOR ALL SAINTS' SUNDAY

Prayer of the Day (Collect)

God of multitudes without number, whose people are knit together in one holy communion: We come before you in the glorious presence of all who have served and in the humility of knowing the many ways we have failed to serve. Grant us grace so to follow your blessed saints in lives of faith and commitment that we may persevere in the course set before us to be living signs of your gospel and, at the last, with all your saints, to share in your eternal joy; through Jesus Christ, to whom with you and the Spirit, one holy God, be honour and praise.

Louise Mangan, 1992

Prayers of Thanksgiving and Intercession

We thank you, God, for the stories of our faith community, so rich a part of our heritage, the tales of dedication and triumphant spirituality in the face of oppression and death. We name the names of the great ones of the faith: Mary, Stephen, Peter, Lydia; early church leaders such as Ignatius and Polycarp; the great mystics: Dame Julian of Norwich, Teresa of Avila. We see Martin Luther forsaking the only world he knew, fired by a vision of the way your church should be. We remember Joan of Arc, Father Brebeuf, Deitrich Bonhoeffer, Martin Luther King, Jr. And we recognize the countless unnamed ones who stand with them. They all believed that your way was the only way, that you would be with them in the darkest hour, that your life was greater than the world's death.

It seems easier, God, to be Christian today. Our lives are not threatened because of our faith. But Jesus warned us about the demonic forces that may spare our bodies but attack our souls. Whenever your church is taken for granted, whenever your Word is put in a box and denied all relevance to daily living, whenever the connection between our abundance and others' poverty is denied, remind us of your saints, O God. Help us to be strong in our dedication to the way of life you would have us lead in *our* time and place, as witnesses to the loving justice you declare as the only way for your children to live.

And never allow us to forget, O God, those faithful ones today who suffer for your cause. In Latin America, in China, even here in Canada: wherever your body is nailed to the cross of injustice, may your people know that our prayers are with them. And may our prayers issue in concrete action, as we do all that we can to support our sisters and brothers in the struggle for justice and for life.

In the name of Jesus, the crucified yet resurrected One, we pray.

Jack Ballantine-Dickson, 1984

God of all goodness and grace, Spirit in whom we live and move and have our being: We thank you that you chose not to exist apart from your world, but sent Jesus, your Love Incarnate, to be light in the world's darkness. We give you thanks that in the Risen Christ we can know you, our God, and worship you in prayer and in action.

We give you thanks, God of the Ages, for that great cloud of witnesses who have gone before us. We stand as your people in succession with women, men, and children of all generations—prophets and priests, apostles and parents, leaders and faithful followers—who have testified to your truth and staked their lives on your vision of a world holy and whole.

In the power of the Holy Spirit who came like wind and fire to make us one, we pray for our sisters and brothers everywhere who continue that witness in our world. Be with those who are persecuted for your name's sake. Be with those who are spending their lives for the sake of your gospel.

God of peace and justice: Enable us to proclaim and live your vision. Abide with us and in us and free us to serve. Give us the will to speak your Word and do your work, to be the people in whom the world may see your new community coming near.

With hearts alive to the mystery of your presence in our world, in ways we can trust but never fully know, we pray to you in the ancient words: Our Father...

Paul Fayter, 1986

Commissioning and Benediction

May you count it joy to be numbered among the saints of God. Go forth to serve God and neighbour in all you do. And the blessing of God the source of Love, of Christ that Love incarnate, and of the Holy Spirit, Love's power, be with you all.

Peter Wyatt, 1989

PRAYERS FOR PEACE SABBATH/ REMEMBRANCE DAY

Prayer of the Day (Collect)

Creator God, gentle in power and strong in tenderness: Kindle, we pray, in the hearts of all people, your passion for peace and your will for justice, that we may fearlessly contend against the powers of death and restrain evil's rage with your love; through Jesus Christ, to whom with you and the Spirit, one holy God, be honour and praise, this day and always.

Louise Mangan, 1992

Calls to Worship

1. We come to worship as those baptized in the name of the Prince of Peace.
2. But we come from a world torn by violence and division.
1. We worship the God who calls and enables us, in the midst of the violence of our world, to live and work for God's vision of justice and shalom.

Nancy Stephenson, 1986

1. God calls us to bring good news to the afflicted, to heal the broken-hearted, to announce release and freedom.
2. We shall beat our swords into ploughshares and our spears into pruning-hooks. Nation shall not lift up sword against nation, neither shall they learn war anymore.
1. Jesus said, "Blessed are the peacemakers, for they shall be called children of God."

2. We gather in the name of the God of peace and justice.

Laura J. Turnbull, 1988

Prayers of Approach and Confession

God of healing and wholeness, we come in worship earnestly desiring peace in our world, not war. We come earnestly desiring peace within our families and communities. We come earnestly desiring peace in our hearts and in our relationship with you. Grant us peace, O God. And help us in this worship to remember and honour those who have lived, and those who have died, for peace.

Lakeview United, Regina, Sask., 1989

Gracious God, on this Remembrance Day we acknowledge the double-edged nature of our remembering. We confess the ultimate evil of war and our part and our society's part in the violence of our world. And yet, with very real gratitude we remember those who sacrificed health and life for freedom from this evil.

Stir us, O God, to hear your Word this Remembrance Day. Strengthen us to work at the unfinished task of proclaiming your peace in the midst of our violent world.

Mark Ferrier, 1991

Holy God, today we remember and repent as we acknowledge the horror of war. Violence and hatred have so often overwhelmed our world. And even in our own lives, hatred has often overcome love and violence has obliterated peace.

Heal our warring madness, God. Assist us as we work for peace in our homes, our community, our church, and our world. Call us again to live lives of love, caring, generosity, and concern. This we ask in the name of Jesus Christ, the Prince of Peace.

Don Daniel, 1990

1. "Come and see what God has done, what amazing things God has done on earth."
2. Amaze us again in our time, O God. Renew in us a vision of your new age dawning, your power to stir, disturb, and call forth new life.

1. "God causes wars to cease throughout the earth, breaking the bow, shattering the spear, throwing the shield into the fire."
2. Give us the foresight to see beyond cruise missiles, ten-megaton bombs, "good guys and bad guys."

1. "Cease your fighting, and know that I am God."
2. Give us peace in our relationships, O God: in our parenting, our partnering, our friendships, our work. Banish from us our angry bruising words, our violent games, our bitter memories.

1. "For God Almighty will be with us; the Holy One of Jacob is our refuge."
2. Draw us back to the well-springs of our faith, O God, to the obedience of the cross, the expectation of Easter, the renewal and power of Pentecost. On this Remembrance Sunday (Peace Sabbath), draw us back to you.

Terry Shillington, 1985

Assurance of Pardon/Forgiveness

The prophets dreamed of the day when we shall beat our swords into ploughshares and our spears into pruning-hooks; nation shall not lift up sword against nation, neither shall they learn war anymore.

Trust the God who longs for peace. We are a people strengthened and empowered to be peacemakers in our world.

Don Daniel, 1990

Prayers of Thanksgiving and Intercession

God of shalom, of justice, peace, freedom, health, and wholeness: creating and re-creating God, we praise your holy name.

We bless you for making covenant with us and calling us into your judgement and grace. You are for us and with us in our greatest joy and our most crushing sorrow. By the power of your love, even death and despair have been defeated.

We long to place our total trust and hope in you. But we are surrounded by violence, caught up in evil forces beyond our control. Fear has gripped us by the throat. With eyes gone blind and ears gone deaf, we cast about for protection, clinging to the false gods of power and security. We have learned to love the very weapons that threaten our lives. Abandoning the unarmed Christ, we have forgotten who and whose we are.

And yet, struggle to trust and hope, O God. For the sake of your Suffering Servant, in the name of the Prince of Peace, help us to put aside our idolatry. Give us the will to beat our swords into ploughshares and our spears into pruning-hooks, to refuse to learn war anymore.

Reconcile us to you, to each other, and to our best selves. Grant us wisdom to perceive you, diligence to follow you, ears to hear you, eyes to behold you. Grant hearts to meditate upon you, hands to serve you, voices to proclaim you. Out of the wells of our silence and the poverty of our love, we express our longing in the words that Jesus taught us....

Paul Fayter, 1985

God of justice and peace, we pray to you from the midst of a world oppressed by darkness. We are caught up in the forces of injustice, prejudice, hatred, and greed that fracture our world and corrode human community. In the midst of our own concerns we have not always sought justice and peace for others. Illumine our hearts, O God. Let your light stream into the dark corners of our living and free us from the power of darkness and sin.... *(silent confession)*

On this Remembrance Day, O God, we are grateful for those who died that we might live, who suffered and still suffer that we might know freedom. Turn our minds and hearts to the determination to live for peace, for the sake of the Prince of Peace, for the sake of every person on the face of this earth, for the sake of all creation.... *(silent prayer)*

In memory of those who died in war, and in the firm and fervent hope of a just and lasting peace in our time, we ask that you pour your gift of healing grace upon us. Draw us close to you, the source of all goodness and love, that we may become whole and holy men and women, young people and children. We ask, believing that you *do* answer, in Jesus' name.

Don Keenliside, 1986

We pray to you, O God, for all people everywhere, that in their need, hidden and manifest, they may be comforted.

We remember that others live where war, violence, and injustice are a fact of daily life. We ask your presence with them in their struggles for justice and peace. And we ask that you be with us that we may better understand their pain and move in our own lives to change what we do that contributes to that pain.

We remember those individuals who actively seek your peace through their commitment and work. Strengthen and uphold them in the task which seems unending. We ask that through your gift of love we may be strengthened to act out our concern for peace in our world.

Finally, God, we remember those in our own families, communities, and country who suffer from violence and injustice, and those who seek to serve them. Help us to be more active in our concern, more giving of our selves and resources, that we may be a strength to your people, a visible and active sign of your peaceable kingdom.

Keep us ever mindful of the peace that is more than the absence of war, the peace that is the presence of justice, equity, love, and right relationship throughout all creation.

Wendy Howie, 1989

Faithful God, on this Remembrance Sunday we remember the men and women who have struggled for peace, who have stood against evil, who have sought justice with their blood, their bodies, their minds, their futures, their lives—in the great European wars, in the wars in Southeast Asia, the Middle East, Southern Africa, Latin America. Hear our prayers as we name those known to us in our hearts, and are thankful.... *(silent prayer)*

Compassionate God, on this Remembrance Sunday we remember those whose lives hold little hope for peace with any kind of security—refugees, the elderly on marginal incomes, people of colour in a world where white is dominant, single mothers with children to feed, the disabled. We remember the people we know whose peace has been shattered by illness and grief, and we name them now.... *(silent prayer)*

Ever-present God, on this Remembrance Sunday

we remember ourselves—sometimes confident, sometimes frightened; sometimes ready to take a stand for justice, sometimes looking for the quickest way out; sometimes conscious of an inner peace, sometimes intensely lonely, unable to feel the reality of you in us or in our world.

Gentle, tender, creator God: Help us remember your constant love. Stubborn, determined Sustainer God, push us to be messengers of peace. We remember the vision of peace that the prophets proclaimed, that Jesus taught, that Ghandi lived for, that Helen Caldicott and Desmond Tutu work for; that we dream of, strive for, long for.

Give us peace in our time, O God. Give us peace in our time.

Caryn Douglas, 1990

We remember, God, the men and women who have served, and fallen, in defence of the sovereignty of nations, the dignity of all people, and the right to be free from domination and oppression. In honour of these fallen we keep silent now, as a foretaste of the silence that will fall when every weapon at last is stilled....

Robin Wardlaw, 1991

The Traditional Act of Remembrance

1. They shall not grow old as we that are left grow old. Age shall not weary them nor the years condemn.
2. At the going down of the sun and in the morning, we will remember them.

    Last Post — Silence — Reveille

1. Eternal rest grant unto them, O God, and may perpetual light shine upon them.
2. May the souls of the righteous, through your great mercy, rest in peace.

S/A, 1990

A Closing Prayer

Bread of life, bread of mercy, bread of hope: We lift our hearts to you in prayer and praise. Mend our broken world, our broken lives.

Across the barriers that divide race from race, class from class, reconcile us, O God, by your cross.

Across the barriers that divide women from men, adults from children, reconcile us, O Christ, by your cross.

Across the barriers that divide people of different faiths, that divide Christian from Christian, reconcile us, O Christ, by your cross.

Creator, Redeemer, Sustainer: Lead us from darkness into light, from death into life, from doubt, despair, and indifference into faith, hope, and life.

And we, as leaves dancing before the wind, shall feel the reeling force of him who soothes the sea and lets the voiceless speak, who dares the dead to rise and delights in all creation, including each of us.

S/A, 1985

Commissionings and Benedictions

We are called not to be peace-lovers, or peace-keepers, but to be peace-makers. Go forth in the name of the Prince of Peace, living and working for that day when God's peaceable kingdom will be a reality.

Jack Ballantine-Dickson, 1984

Go in peace to be bearers of peace. And the peace of our Saviour Christ be with us all.

Don Robertson, 1991

PRAYERS FOR THE SOVEREIGNTY OF CHRIST SUNDAY

Prayer of the Day (Collect)

Tender God, voice of the voiceless and power of the powerless: Bind us together in the unceasing love of your anointed one, our servant king, who heals our hearts to show us the way. We pray in Christ's name; to whom with you and the Spirit, one holy God, be honour and praise, this day and forever.

Louise Mangan, 1992

Call to Worship

1. "I am the Alpha and the Omega," says almighty God, who is, and was, and is to come.
2. Blessing and honour, glory and power be unto God!
1. Worthy is Christ, the Lamb who was slain, to receive glory and honour and power.
2. To the One who sits on the throne, and to the Lamb be blessing and honour, glory and power, forever and ever. Amen.

Don Daniel, 1990

Prayers of Thanksgiving and Intercession

Praise to you, O God, whose reign of love and justice we pray for daily. Praise to you, O Christ, whose kingdom we catch glimpses of, whose dominion will one day change the world, whose new community will never be destroyed.

We thank you, God, for eyes to see the world as it really is, and for hearts and faith enough to believe the world can be transformed. When we look around our world, we are troubled, angered, saddened. So much cries out to be put right; so many cry out for food and shelter, peace and freedom, healing and friendship. Thank you for people of all faiths—and of no faith—but with faith enough to work to make the world a better place.

God, we lift to you our prayers for those who are poor and oppressed—even those who seem rich and free and are not aware of their poverty and oppression. We pray for victims of every form of violence, even those who perpetrate violence. Grant hope. Grant that we, your church, may be agents of liberation and reconciliation. May your love increase, may joy bound, may peace prevail.

And we name, O God, the prayers which are in our hearts, remembering those who have special need of our concern.... *(silence)*

We ask these things in the name of Jesus the Sovereign One, who taught us all to pray....

Paul Fayter, 1992

A PRAYER FOR LATE EVENING WORSHIP

Holy One, as in the night you freed your people from slavery and led them to freedom in a promised land, so, in this night, free us from bondage to the past and to our daily cares and worries and bring us forth to a new life of faithfulness.

Holy One, as in the night you entered our history in the helplessness of a little child, so, in this night, enter our helplessness and cause us to be present to your world.

Holy One, as in the night you shattered the chains of sin and death and raised up Jesus to life, so, in this night, break the shackles which bind us and bring us to light and new life.

Father/Mother, Christ, and Spirit, breathe into us your healing breath and claim us again for your own.

Lynnette Miller, 1986

Chapter Three

Preparing for Congregational Worship

Help! Our minister is away, and we're responsible for Sunday worship!

Preparing for Sunday morning worship is both a simple and complex task: simple in that, with the investment of a few hours' time and a bit of creativity and care, any team of four or five people can do it; complex because to prepare the Sunday service week after week is to lead the congregation, on an ongoing basis, in the most important activity the church engages in—the worship of God. And that takes commitment, special gifts, training, and a considerable array of resources.

This chapter is specifically for those who have agreed to prepare a Sunday service because their minister is away. What follows is a step by step guide for preparing Sunday worship.

STEP 1: Choose a Worship Team

Gather a team of four or five people, including the music person for your congregation, a teenager, and somebody who "has a way with children." If at all possible, find these people at least three weeks in advance of the Sunday on which you have agreed to lead worship. The process will involve two team meetings plus a certain amount of phoning back and forth in between.

STEP 2: Gather Resources

If this is a special Sunday or season of the church year, look up the background material in *Worship for All Seasons* ("About Advent," "About Lent," "About Pentecost," etc.). Copy for all team members.

Look up the lectionary readings for the Sunday in question (see the most recent copy of *Gathering*, pages 3-4). If your congregation does not use the lectionary, discuss with your minister before he or she goes away what readings might be appropriate.

Obtain copies (one for each team member) of the lectionary background material from *The Whole People of God (WPG)* curriculum (the blue sheet, "Biblical Background"). If your congregation does not use *WPG*, ask your minister for some other lectionary resource, or borrow a copy of the *WPG* material from a neighbouring congregation.

Send copies of all this material to each member of the worship team. Ask them to read the scripture passages and the background material in preparation for your first meeting.

Ask each team member to come to the meeting with as short a statement as possible (one word, or a very short sentence) about what they think the central mood or theme of the service might be. This statement should arise out of the sense of the season, one or more of the scripture readings, or the season and scripture together. Examples:

> Advent: Expectation
> Lent: Journey to the cross
> Parable of the Good Samaritan:
>   What does it mean to be a neighbour?
> God's call to Samuel/Jesus' calling of the
>   disciples: How does God call us today?
> I Corinthians 13: Love is....

It might be helpful to copy this instruction and include it in your packet of resources for the team members.

STEP 3: The First Meeting

Have on hand:

- a Bible (to settle arguments!)
- copies of *The Hymn Book, Songs for a Gospel People*, or whatever music resource(s) your congregation uses;
- several examples of recent Sunday bulletins;
- a large flip chart and flow pens, or a large blackboard and chalk;
- copies of this chapter, one for each team member,

so that people can follow along, step by step, as you plan.

Before the meeting, and in keeping with your normal Sunday bulletin, outline the order of service on the flip chart or blackboard. Leave lots of space between each item for "filling in the blanks."

Begin the meeting with prayer:

Bless, O God, our time together as we prepare to lead your people in worship. Bless us and what we do, that we may be a blessing to your people; we pray in Jesus' name. Amen.

Establish the mood/theme of the service:

Have each team member share her or his statement of mood/theme. Write these on the flip chart or blackboard as they are shared.

Discuss the various suggestions for a few moments. Is there one mood or theme that seems to be emerging? Resist the temptation to combine everybody's suggestions for the sake of consensus, however. And keep it simple! Choose between the different moods/themes suggested, but keep the discussion going until all are satisfied with the statement chosen.

Write the agreed upon mood/theme in capital letters in the space marked "Sermon" in the outlined order of worship (this may, in fact, become the title of the sermon).

In all that follows, keep referring back to your statement of mood/theme. This will be your guiding principle!

Gain a sense of the overall order of worship:

Sunday worship is like a drama in three or four acts, depending on the order you use. The titles of these acts (which may already be printed in the order of service) may be something like this:

Act I: Approach
Act II: Word
Act III: Response

or

Act I: Gathering
Act II: Service of the Word
Act III: Service of the Table
Act IV: Going Forth

(The three-act structure follows the order of the 1969 *Service Book;* the four-act structure is based on the 1984 *A Sunday Liturgy.* See volume 1, chapter 1, of *Worship for All Seasons* if you want to know more about these two slightly different worship orders.)

Each act in the overall drama of worship is related to those which precede and follow. There is a natural "flow," then, in worship, from one act to the next. This flow could be described as:

• We approach God in praise and confession;
• God speaks to us in scripture, story, and sermon;
• we respond to God's Word by offering our gifts and our prayers for others, and by going forth to serve.

or

• We gather as a worshipping community;
• God speaks to us in scripture, story, and sermon and we respond with prayers for others;
• we present our gifts at the Lord's table and offer our prayers of thanksgiving;
• God sends us forth to love and serve.

Discuss this dramatic flow to worship. Can you see it in the worship order of your congregation?

If titles are not already included in your order of worship, you may want to name the various "acts" in the drama. Write these titles in the appropriate spots on your outlined worship order (or underline them if they are already there).

Now you are ready to begin working on the individual elements which together make up the drama of Sunday worship. Remember, however, to keep in mind your central mood or theme!

Plan the Word:

On non-sacramental Sundays (which we presume this is, as your minister is away), the Word section of the service is usually seen as the central act in the drama of worship. So we begin our detailed planning there.

1. Scripture Readings

Some congregations use all three readings provided by the lectionary, plus a psalm, in the following order: Old Testament, Psalm, New Testament, Gospel. Others use only two readings and a psalm: Old Testament, Psalm, New Testament.

Choose the readings you are going to use. Write your choices in the appropriate spaces on your outlined order of worship.

If the psalm is normally printed and read responsively, assign someone to do this. Do not be afraid to edit for length and appropriateness. The psalm (which was, in fact, the "hymn book" of the Hebrew people) is normally seen as a response to the Old Testament reading. Try to hold on to that sense of responding to the first reading as you do your editing.

2. Time with the Children

If a "Time with the Children" or "Children's Story" is included in your order of worship, decide how you are going to do this.

Suggestion 1: Some congregations use the "Theme Conversation in Church" from the *WPG* curriculum (blue sheet, second page). If your congregation uses *WPG*, assign someone to obtain the material and prepare to lead the children's time.

Suggestion 2: If your congregation does not use *WPG*, but one of the scripture passages is an appropriate story, tell it as a story during the children's time. A few pictures or simple objects might help in the telling. (The old "New Curriculum" materials, stored away in many church basements, are full of excellent "teaching pictures.")

Suggestion 3: Prepare one of the scripture passages as a dramatic reading. Gather a few children ahead of time, rehearse the reading, and use it in place of the regular reading of scripture. (Do some thinking about how the children are going to be heard; the use of microphones, etc.) You might then gather the children during the Time with the Children and discuss what the story was all about. Try to avoid moralizing or "making a point," however. Discuss what was happening in the story, how people felt, what difference the action in the story made in people's lives or in the life of their community.

Suggestion 4: Choose the scripture passage that best underlines the mood/theme chosen for the service. Talk a bit about the mood/theme in terms the children will understand. Teach a song that supports this mood/theme (see comments on "Children's Hymn," page 87 of this chapter).

3. Sermon

Now we come to the part everyone has been dreading: Who is going to preach the sermon? But preaching doesn't need to be all that daunting, especially if you only have to do it once in a while. (And think in terms of eight to twelve minutes, rather than the traditional fifteen to twenty!)

Suggestion 1: Build on the "Time with the Children." How does what was discussed with the children relate to adults? to the life of your congregation? to the life of your community? Maybe forget about preaching here and simply make a few comments, ask a few questions, and have a discussion (a "Time with the Adults" just like the "Time with the Children"!)

Suggestion 2: The Biblical Background (blue sheet) in the *WGP* curriculum begins with an Outline of the Theme (the opening paragraph) and then relates each of the lectionary readings to the theme. If the statement of mood/theme chosen by the worship team is similar to that of the *WPG*, the *WPG* material might be the basis for the sermon. Of further help will be the corresponding material in the *WPG* Adult Study Pak, especially the comments on the various scripture passages in the Adult Pak Lesson Plan.

(Note: Do not feel that you have to deal with all three scripture readings on any given Sunday. One scripture passage may be particularly appropriate. Dealing with it alone may be sufficient. Better that the sermon be too short than too long!)

Suggestion 3: If the scripture passages all relate to your chosen theme, the sermon might be presented by three people rather than by one. Assign each person one of the scripture readings. Have one person introduce the theme to the congregation, and then each of the three, in turn, takes (no more than) three minutes to make one or two comments about how their particular scripture passage relates to the theme. Each person concludes with a sentence or two about what difference this would make in our lives personally, as a congregation, or as a larger community.

Decide who is going to do the sermon and how it is going to be done.

Plan the music:

The obvious person to be in charge of planning the music for the service is the organist or choir director of your congregation. In a couple of instances, however, it will be useful to have input from those responsible for other elements in the service.

Choose who will plan the music. The following suggestions may be helpful.

1. Hymns

Typically, there are four hymns in the Sunday service: a Hymn of Praise, Children's Hymn, Hymn of Response (hymn after the sermon), and Hymn of Going Forth. Each has a different function in the drama of worship.

Hymn of Praise: Except perhaps in Lent, when the mood of worship is more subdued, the first hymn in the service of worship should be a resounding hymn of praise. Hymns no. 1-71, 81-90, and 357-362 in *The Hymn Book* (hymns no. 72-80 if the season is Lent), are all appropriate. Similar praise-type hymns may be found in *Songs for a Gospel People*. If this is a special season in the church year, however, check the hymns listed in the Table of Contents of *The Hymn Book* under the section entitled "The Christian Year."

Children's Hymn: This hymn needs to be chosen in conjunction with the person preparing the Time With the Children. The *WPG* curriculum suggests appropriate hymns for each Sunday (blue sheet, bottom of second page). *All God's Children Sing* has both a theme index (page 98) and a biblical index (page 99) which might be helpful. Be sure that the children know the hymn, or plan on adequate time in the service for teaching it.

Hymn of Response: The hymn after the sermon is normally seen as a response to the theme of the sermon itself. The hymn needs to be chosen, then, in conversation with whoever is responsible for the sermon.

Suggestion 1: The current issue of *Gathering* includes hymn selections for each Sunday (see the section "Sunday by Sunday").

Suggestion 2: The Hymn Book has both a table of contents at the front, in which the hymns are listed according to theme, and a subject index at the back. Choose the theme or subject closest to that of the sermon and check the hymns suggested.

Suggestion 3: If you look under "P" in the subject index of *The Hymn Book*, you will find a listing of hymns based on various scripture passages. *Songs for a Gospel People* also has a biblical index at the back. Echoing the central scripture passage in song, after the sermon, is a helpful way to tie the Service of the Word together.

Hymn of Going Forth: The final hymn of the service should be a rousing hymn of faith, sending us forth in style ("Guide me, O thou great Jehovah" comes to mind). Hymns no. 263-309 in *The Hymn Book*, and similar "going forth" hymns in *Songs for a Gospel People*, are appropriate. Try to avoid using a little-known hymn as the final hymn of the service; let the Hymn of Going Forth be one that the people enjoy singing!

(Note: If someone other than the music person is choosing the hymns, check with those who know to make sure that the tunes are familiar to the congregation!)

2. Choir Anthem

Sometimes an anthem is inserted between two of the scripture readings; sometimes it is sung after the children have left for Sunday school, immediately before the sermon.

When possible, the anthem should support the mood or theme of the service. Is there an anthem that would be particularly appropriate on this occasion? (See the current issue of *Gathering*, the section entitled "Sunday by Sunday," for suggestions.)

3. Service Music

Service music is all those sung bits and pieces repeated Sunday by Sunday at various points in the order of worship. Sometimes these remain constant throughout the year; sometimes they change with the seasons and festival days. Examples of service music your congregation may use are as follows:

Introit: Some congregations begin their worship

with a set one- or two-verse hymn, sung by the choir or choir and congregation together (the traditional United Church introit was the first and last verses of "Holy, holy, holy..."). Recently, some congregations have begun changing their introits to match the seasons of the church year (the first verse of "O come, O come, Emmanuel" in Advent; verses 1 and 3 of "That Eastertide with joy was bright" on the Sundays after Easter; etc.)

Kyrie eleison: A Kyrie eleison (or Agnus Dei) is sometimes sung as part of the act of confession (see the box on page 28 of this volume for a description of how the Kyrie might be used). Four different Kyries are offered in *Songs for a Gospel People* (3, 25, 35, 51).

Doxology: Doxologies are one-verse hymns of praise addressed to the Trinity (see *The Hymn Book* no. 197, verse 3; no. 361, verse 5; *Songs for a Gospel People* no. 11). The traditional United Church doxology was "Praise God from whom all blessings flow...." Doxologies are used either as a response to the Assurance of Forgiveness, or as a burst of praise as the offering is brought forth to the Table. Doxologies are sung standing to emphasize our joy in praising God.

The Lord's Prayer (sung), either at the conclusion of the Prayers of Thanksgiving and Intercession or the Thanksgiving and Dedication (offertory) Prayer.

Three-fold Amen (or some other concluding song), sung immediately after the Benediction.

Any service music used in your congregation has undoubtedly already been established and does not require any decision-making on the part of the worship team. Service music is one of the most important elements of worship, however, as it provides anchor-points—familiar to the congregation—throughout the service.

Mark in or circle the service music on your outlined order of worship.

Plan the prayers:

It is probably simplest if you, as team leader, are responsible for planning the prayers. There is one prayer, however, that might be assigned to one of the other members of the team: the Prayers of Thanksgiving and Intercession or Prayers of the People (depending on which format you use).

Assign this prayer to a team member. (See the boxes on pages 32 and 36 of this volume for background material on these prayers. The appropriate volume of *Worship for All Seasons*, or the current issue of *Gathering*, will provide examples.)

Suggestion: Ask the youth group or several teenagers to write and lead this prayer. You might discover a new perspective on praying!

Some congregations follow the Prayers of Thanksgiving and Intercession with the Lord's Prayer, either said or sung. Check on this and make sure that whoever is leading the prayers at this point is prepared to move along into the Lord's Prayer if that is your congregation's practice.

So, that's enough for the first meeting—it has probably been a long session. Take courage, however! The major work has all been assigned. At your next meeting, the various elements of the service will fall into place. Check, before you go, that everybody understands the tasks they have agreed to do before the next meeting.

End the meeting by standing together and singing one of the traditional evening hymns (*The Hymn Book*, no. 366, "The day thou gavest, Lord, is ended") and then join hands and repeat together the Mizpah Benediction (the most ancient parting formula in the Bible, Genesis 31:49):

*May the Lord watch between you and me,
while we are absent, one from the other.*

STEP 4: (Between meetings) Planning the Prayers

The shorter prayers throughout the service are normally led by one person, sometimes called the Presider (or Worship Leader). This person does not dominate the service, but acts, in a sense, as the conductor of the orchestra, providing unity and coherence to the congregation's worship. The suggestion is that you would be that person, and therefore are responsible for choosing and leading the prayers.

The prayers are as follows (the Call to Worship/Greeting and Versicle, and the Commissioning-Benediction, are not strictly prayers, but are included in this list for the sake of simplicity):

1. Call to Worship/Greeting and Versicle

Some congregations begin the spoken part of the Sunday service with a Call to Worship; others use the apostolic Greeting, "The grace of our Saviour Christ...," sometimes followed by a seasonal versicle (the boxes on pages 22 and 24 of this volume explain the difference).

Choose a Call or Greeting and Versicle from the appropriate volume of *Worship for All Seasons* or the current issue of *Gathering*. Remember to take into account the season of the church year and/or the theme of the service. If the Call or Greeting and Versicle are designed to be read responsively (i.e., designated 1..., 2...), they must be printed in the order of worship.

2. Prayer of Approach/Prayer of the Day

Depending on which format you use, a Prayer of Approach or Prayer of the Day follows the Call or Greeting (the boxes on pages 22 and 26 explain the difference). Choose a prayer from the appropriate volume of *Worship for All Seasons* or the current issue of *Gathering*.

3. Prayer of Confession/Assurance of Forgiveness

Some congregations omit the Confession except in the season of Lent. If your congregation includes a time of confession, however, choose a Prayer of Confession and Assurance of Forgiveness from the appropriate volume of *Worship for All Seasons* or current issue of *Gathering* (the box on page 28 of this volume outlines a useful order for the act of confession).

The Prayer of Confession is usually printed in the order of worship and said in unison; the Assurance is either led by the worship leader alone (not printed) or said responsively (and therefore must be printed).

4. Prayer for Illumination

Often, immediately before the sermon, the person preaching will lead in a brief moment of prayer. The classic Prayer for Illumination is:

May the words of my mouth, and the meditations of our hearts and minds, be acceptable in your sight, O Lord, our Rock and our Redeemer.

This prayer is led, of course, by whoever is doing the sermon. They should therefore have the final say as to what the prayer is going to be. A selection of Prayers for Illumination is found on page 40, vol. 1, of *Worship for All Seasons*.

5. Announcements

These are normally printed in the bulletin. Some congregations do the announcements immediately before the service begins, others at some other point in the service. (Placing the announcements immediately before the Prayers of Intercession/Prayers of the People seems logical—the announcements about our church life and concerns in the community are made just before we pray for the church and the world.)

Wherever they come in the service, it is probably sufficient to draw people's attention to the announcements as printed (though make sure that any which involve children or seniors, who may have difficulty reading, are spoken aloud). Conclude by asking if anybody has any further announcements to make.

6. Prayers of Thanksgiving and Intercession/ Prayers of the People

These prayers have been discussed and assigned as above.

7. Offertory Prayer/Prayers of Thanksgiving and Dedication

In some congregations, the Offertory Prayer is said before the offering is gathered; more usually it is said after the gifts have been brought forward and the offertory song sung (while those who have gathered the offerings are standing before the Table).

Check how your congregation does this and work out in your mind the mechanics of receiving the offering and leading the prayer. (Note that this prayer is usually led from behind the Table and not from the pulpit or lectern.)

Those congregations that follow *A Sunday Liturgy* format combine the Prayers of Thanksgiving with the Prayer of Dedication (usually followed by the Lord's Prayer).

Choose an Offertory Prayer or Prayer of Thanksgiving and Dedication from the appropriate volume of *Worship for All Seasons* or current issue of *Gathering*.

8. Commissioning and Benediction

The final act of worship is that of being sent forth and blessed on our way by the Commissioning and Benediction. These are most dramatically offered by standing, hands outstretched, in front of the communion table.

Choose a Commissioning and Benediction from the appropriate volume of *Worship for All Seasons* or current issue of *Gathering*. If the Benediction is normally followed by a sung Three-fold Amen (or other song of departing), provide a copy of the Benediction to the organist so that he or she knows when to come in.

STEP 5: The Second Meeting

Again, begin with prayer:

Continue to be with us, God, as we plan together this evening. Guide and bless what we do, that our planning might bear fruit in worship worthy of you; we pray in Jesus' name. Amen.

Reporting back:

Have those who were assigned tasks at your first meeting report on their progress.

1. Write in the hymn numbers and title of the anthem on the outlined order of worship. Make sure that you have copies of any service music for including in the order of worship according to your congregation's practice.

2. Obtain a copy of the psalm so that it might be printed in the order of worship. Decide on who and how the scripture passages are going to be read.

3. Share with the team the prayers you have chosen. Have the person or people responsible for the Prayers of Thanksgiving and Intercession/Prayers of the People share their progress so far. Discuss the mechanics of how these prayers are going to be led (see the box on page 36 of this volume for suggestions).

4. Encourage those responsible for the children's time and the sermon to discuss their thinking so far. Saying things out loud helps ideas gel and ensures that the entire team stays on board as the planning progresses.

Plan the mechanics of the service:

What else needs to be done? Arranging for the church to be open Sunday morning? Microphones/sound system? Greeters and ushers? People to take up the offering? Somebody to arrange for coffee after the service? Consider all the little details and make arrangements accordingly.

Rehearse, either tonight or early Sunday morning:

Walk through the service so that everyone knows what they are doing and when, where they are standing, what microphone they are going to use, etc. Rehearsing beforehand not only ensures that the service will flow more smoothly, but also lowers the anxiety level of all concerned.

Conclude the meeting with an evening hymn: (*The Hymn Book*, no. 370, "Saviour, again to thy dear name we raise") and the Mizpah Benediction, as before.

STEP 6: Final Details

Prepare the Order of Service and ensure that sufficient copies are printed.

On Sunday morning, immediately before worship begins, gather with the worship team (and the choir) and offer prayer:

Be in our minds, and on our lips, and in our hearts, gracious God, as we lead your people in worship. Fill us with your Spirit, that this time of worship may truly be a blessing. This we pray in Jesus' name. Amen.

May God be with you as you lead your congregation in worship!